LEADING SCHOOLS IN
TIMES OF CHANGE

'This is a superbly balanced book at the cutting edge of writing on school leadership. The issues addressed are international in scope so the book will have wide appeal wherever efforts are being made to create world class schools. We know that schools must build a capacity to ensure that the needs of all students are addressed and that leadership is critically important in building that capacity. This book shows how it can be done by drawing on the rich experience of all players in schools which have achieved success. It is an honest book because it faces up to the tensions and dilemmas of leadership. It is a "must read" for policy makers, practitioners, researchers and students who seek to be at the forefront of knowledge on school leadership.'

Professor Brian Caldwell, Dean of Education, University of Melbourne

'*Leading Schools in Times of Change* tells the story of leadership and the moral authority that makes it effective. Arguing that joining the values of the heart with responsiveness to societal and political realities is key. The authors find that effective heads of schools base their practice on ideas and have the grit to act on these ideas. Richly illustrated by the voices of heads and those they lead, leadership grows up in this book. A must read for anyone serious about improving schools.'

Thomas J. Sergiovanni is the Lillian Radford Professor of Education and Administration at Trinity University, USA and author of *The Lifeworld of Leadership: Creating Culture, Community, and Personal Meaning in Our Schools.*

LEADING SCHOOLS IN TIMES OF CHANGE

Christopher Day, Alma Harris,
Mark Hadfield, Harry Tolley
and John Beresford

OPEN UNIVERSITY PRESS
Maidenhead · Philadelphia

Open University Press
McGraw-Hill House
Shoppenhangers Road
Maidenhead
Berkshire
England
SL6 2QL

email: enquiries@openup.co.uk
world wide web: www.openup.co.uk

and
325 Chestnut Street
Philadelphia, PA 19106, USA

First Published 2000
Reprinted 2003

A catalogue record of this book is available from the British Library

ISBN 0335 20582 8 (pb) 0335 20583 6 (hb)

Library of Congress Cataloging-in-Publication Data
Leading schools in times of change / Christopher Day . . . [et al.].
    p. cm.
Includes bibliographical references (p.) and index.
ISBN 0-335-20583-6 (hb)   ISBN 0-335-20582-8 (pb)
    1. Educational leadership – Great Britain. 2. School management
and organization – Great Britain. 3. Educational change – Great
Britain. I. Day, Christopher, ACP.
LB2900.5.L45   2000
371.2′00941–dc21   99-050029

Typeset by Graphicraft Limited, Hong Kong
Printed in Great Britain by Ashford Colour Press Ltd., Gosport, Hants.

CONTENTS

PREFACE

In a climate of educational policy that tends to promote a mechanistic, rationalistic view of leadership, this book provides a refreshing and rigorous, evidence-based view of the challenges, joys and headaches of being a successful headteacher at the beginning of the twenty-first century. The 'values-led contingency' model which it identifies confirms that the role of the head is intricately complex and depends upon balancing the demands of external pressures, internal priorities and personal and professional needs. Just as there are ways in which some pupils learn best – but not all pupils, and not all of the time – so there are ways in which schools can be led – but not one way. Key to successful leadership, however, is getting the values right and having the right values in order to manage the tensions and dilemmas with which leaders must live.

One of the common threads that emerges from the research upon which this book is based is the need for heads to be 'ahead of the game', aware of the tugs and pulls within and without the school organization, and be able to act on that information. Perhaps that defines one of the essential differences between leadership and management. Management without leadership may well be more tolerant of organizational or personal imperfections. Having skills of leadership can transform weaknesses and move a school on. However, while management without leadership is an option, leadership without management is not. Successful schools have taken the imposed agenda and made it fit their organization. How to incorporate new ideas without either drowning teachers in additional work, or simply paying lip service to change has been one of the tensions of the past decade. Get the balance wrong, and you end up with burnt out teachers, stress based backlash, or a façade which cracks under systematic scrutiny.

The greatest criticism of external change wrought on schools is that it fails to take account of 'the real world' out here, every day, in the classroom. One of the most welcome facets of this work is that it is a complete synthesis between the worlds of academia and practice. The study is firmly grounded and comes at a time when teachers are in dire need of good news. This book is full of it, and while it centres upon schools with a track record of success, it contains vignettes of practice that we can all recognize. The stories are told with a detailed and intelligent empathy that has been so much lacking in the headline culture of the recent past. This book is a tribute to the 'commitment, qualities and industry' of headteachers, deputies, and their staff that is long overdue.

Mick Brookes
President, National Association of Headteachers

FOREWORD

Because of its relatively lengthy experience with New Right or neo Conservative (and now 'new Labour') education policies being widely adopted by governments in many parts of the world, the United Kingdom is a fertile context for research on school leadership. We find reflected in that context not only mature expressions of those forms of leadership that governments consider to be consistent with their visions for education, but also evidence of the consequences of putting such forms of leadership into practice.

According to one recent analyst,[1] education policy in England has now moved, thanks to its Labour Government, beyond a 1988–1996 'market' phase, to an 'excellence' phase. The market phase was concerned primarily with efficient use of resources, teacher and pupil performance, expanded educational provision, greater choice for parents, greater autonomy for schools to compete for students and greater accountability of schools to their many stakeholders.

The more recent excellence phase has retained many of these same concerns, but with greater emphasis on the attainment of excellence, often through the implementation of government-generated programmes such as the national literacy and national numeracy strategies. This is a highly interventionist and pre-scriptive policy environment for schools. Its purpose is to raise student standards by more or less directly improving the performance of teachers. Increasingly, heads are being viewed as critical to the success of this education agenda.

Curiously, to my mind, while New Right educational policies and their spin-offs aim to produce what the private sector refers to as 'high performance systems',[2] the image of school leadership embedded in those policies flies in the face of all that we know about forms of leadership capable of developing and maintaining such systems. Relevant UK documents, as the authors of this book show, advocate a hierarchical, transactional, control-oriented model of school leadership. So, although the book is written primarily with a UK audience in mind, it is of much wider significance. The book needs to be read by all those with an interest in what it means to offer effective school leadership in a policy context which includes, on the one hand, highly prescriptive external standards and significant accountability demands and, on the other, the need to meet legitimate local needs and build on the capacities of increasingly well-trained professional educators.

While the book engages a large corpus of the existing literature on school leadership, especially in the introductory and concluding chapters, its central contributions are based on the collection of new, qualitative evidence about the effective leadership of 12 headteachers. Two features of the design used for this research have an especially significant bearing on the nature of the results and their use. First, what we learn about the nature of effective school leadership from this study is based on evidence of such leadership not just from the leaders themselves or from their teachers, the two sources used in an overwhelming proportion of previous school leadership research. Rather, the portrait of effective leadership painted by this study is a composite drawn not only from the usual sources, but also from parents, governors, deputy heads, support staff, and *students* (imagine!).

Now I really like this aspect of the study's design because leadership is most usefully thought of as an attribution, or a construction, on the part of its recipients. If a person doesn't experience leadership, there isn't any. Put differently, people volunteer to be followers because of the influence they experience from someone or the group to whom, as a result, they award the designation 'leader'. Because leadership is an individually constructed experience on the part of followers, there is often as much variation in quantitative measures of leadership within schools as there is between schools. This can be explained either by differences in the leadership practices of the head in response to different needs of followers, and/or differences in how the same leadership practices on the part of the head are perceived and interpreted by followers.

What all this complexity boils down to is this. Data collected about effective school leadership from heads tells us what heads think they do that accounts for their effectiveness: this is what Donald Schön would refer to as their 'theory of action'.[3] Data collected from teachers about effective heads' leadership tells us something about how well the head's practices conform to teachers' mental models of what leaders do: their leader prototypes.[4] Neither of these perspectives can be assumed to capture what it is about the head's work that is perceived, for example, by students or parents as helpful to them. So we cannot know what it means to offer effective leadership to these critical stakeholders unless we include them as sources of data in our research. This study achieves what has rarely previously been attempted.

Surprisingly, in the light of the potential variation in perceptions of heads' leadership, evidence from these different sources of information about heads' leadership painted a remarkably consistent picture of what these people do and, even more important as it turns out, why they do it. Perhaps effective leadership includes being especially reflective about your own practices, and better able than most to judge how they will be perceived by others. Perhaps it also means being especially consistent with all stakeholders, and ensuring that such consistency is understood.

A second feature of the research design for this study that I want to comment on concerns the procedure used in selecting the 12 schools included in the study. This procedure aimed to maximize variation in school size, type and location. So the study was conducted in small, rural, primary schools; large, urban, secondary schools; and many variations in between. As a consequence of this sampling procedure, which was itself influenced by the available resources with which to conduct the study, its results capture those aspects of effective leadership *common* to heads across most school types, as distinct from the *full set* of characteristics of, for example, effective primary heads or effective secondary heads.

But we know that school size and type, not to mention the nature of the student body, are significant determinants of the forms of leadership that are helpful to a school. So the characteristics of effective leadership captured by this study ought to be interpreted as a necessary but not sufficient description of what it is that effective school leaders do and why they do it. I highlight this to make the point that such common features of effective school leadership are of enormous value in the design of leadership development programmes. Because these never have enough time to address the full array of potentially useful objectives, choices have to be made. And the results of this study narrow attention to an especially worthwhile set of choices for leadership development purposes. Programme designers – read carefully.

What are these common features of effective school leadership? As the authors make clear in the first chapter, they expected to find support for a transformational orientation to school leadership. This is a form of leadership focused on building the capacities and commitments of staff in the school in the interests of students. Results of the study do indicate that this form of leadership encompassed a significant proportion but not all of what effective heads did, especially the importance attributed to building a shared vision and strong organizational culture.

But few descriptions of transformational leadership to date devote the kind of attention warranted by the authors' data to the central importance of a core set of personal and professional values and an ability to manage competing sets of tensions and dilemmas, helping to explain what it is that effective school leaders do. Values include, for example, a high degree of respect and caring for individuals in the school, as well as a strong sense of fairness, integrity, and honesty in relationships with other people.[5] Nor do many other treatments of transformational leadership touch on a set of personal traits the effective heads in this study shared in common; such traits as enthusiasm, energy, persistence, and calmness in the face of emotionally charged events.

The addition of these values and traits greatly enriches our understandings of what transformational leadership can mean in practice. It does this by clarifying what it is that triggers potential followers' attributions of such leadership. While teachers, governors, students and others can only 'see' the head's behaviour, they are greatly influenced by what they infer to be the causes of that behaviour. And, although the authors themselves do not raise this matter, their data would seem to suggest that the strength of the relationship between leaders and those he or she serves depends critically on the development of trust.

When we judge people to be principled, committed to a vision we also value, to respect our contributions, and to be willing to work tirelessly on behalf of our organization, we trust them to do the right thing. When a school gets to the point where trust is mutual – teachers trust students, parents trust teachers, governors trust heads – then rules become largely unnecessary, and the full capacity of the school's members can be unleashed on behalf of its mission. This is what those advocating hierarchical, control-oriented, transactional forms of leadership for schools seem not to understand. There can never be enough rules to ensure that those we do not trust do the right thing. And as rules are added to prevent more and more anticipated future diversions from the right thing, we inadvertently constrain people from using their problem-solving capacities on behalf of the organization's purposes. Our schools become (or remain), to use Morgan's metaphor, organizations 'with brains'[6] all of which reside at the top of the organization attempting the futile task of thinking for everyone else, and thereby ensuring a low performing system. Mutual trust, in contrast, provides the conditions needed for schools to act 'as brains' – to act so that the intelligence of the organization is dispersed widely and all members of the organization think on its behalf. This is an essential feature of high performing systems. People capable of engendering trust in our schools, as well as building professional commitments and capacities, are the leaders we need if our schools are to become the high performing systems we all dream about. This book makes a significant contribution to our understanding of the qualities those in, and aspiring to, school leader roles need to possess and to further develop.

Kenneth Leithwood
Centre for Leadership Development
Ontario Institute for Studies in Education
University of Toronto

Notes

1. Bell, L. (1999) Back to the future: the development of educational policy in England, *Journal of Educational Administration*, 37(3): 200–28.

2. Lawler, E. (1986) *High involvement management*. San Francisco: Jossey-Bass.
3. Schön, D. (1984) *The Reflective Practitioner*. San Francisco: Jossey-Bass.
4. Leithwood, K. and Jantzi, D. (1998) Explaining variations in teachers' perceptions of principals' leadership: a replication, *Journal of Educational Administration*, 35(3/4): 312–31.
5. For similar evidence see Leithwood, K. and Steinbach, R. (1995) *Expert Problem Solving: Evidence from School and District Leaders*. Albany, NY: SUNY Press.
6. Morgan, G. (1986) *Images of Organization*. Beverly Hills, CA: Sage Publications.

ACKNOWLEDGEMENTS

We wish to acknowledge the NAHT for its foresight in commissioning the study, Wendy James for her tireless work in producing the final manuscript, and the considerable co-operation, openness, frankness, honesty and trust of the headteachers, governors, teachers, ancillaries, parents and students who provided the insights which made possible the original research on which this book is based.

INTRODUCTION

This book is about effective management and leadership in schools. It considers effective leadership from the perspectives of the headteachers, teachers, students, ancillaries, parents and governors in a variety of schools of different phases, locations and size. All the schools had in common not only a reputation for effectiveness among their constituencies but also the fact that they had been adjudged effective through a range of independent indicators including external inspection reports. All had consistently raised student achievement levels – in this sense they were 'improving' schools – and all the headteachers were recognized as being instrumental in this and in the overall success of the schools. In setting out to make sense of contemporary effective school leadership, we did not expect to find convergence or consensus of views between, for example, those in small rural primary school communities and those in inner city secondary schools. It was all the more surprising, then, when the data revealed overwhelming agreement across constituencies and schools as to the features and contexts of effective leadership. What surprised us, also, was that while the mosaic which emerged had echoes in existing leadership literature internationally, it was more complex.

Management and leadership are essential components of headteachers' roles and effective heads need to be able to do both well. They need to engage in people-centred leadership, constantly creating, maintaining, reviewing and renewing the learning and achievement cultures for students, staff and the close communities of parents and governors whom they serve; and they need to model this in the many thousands of daily interactions through which common visions, expectations, standards, relationships and definitions of effectiveness are formed, framed, supported and tested. Of equal importance is their ability to create and monitor organizational structures appropriate to the fulfilment of the legitimate interests and aspirations of both internal and external stakeholders. It follows that effective heads have a major responsibility both for the ongoing, evolutionary development of the schools in which they work and, within this, the more formal accelerated learning opportunities and challenges collectively known as 'school improvement' and 'teacher development'.

We believe that the research study upon which this book is based (commissioned by NAHT, the National Association of Headteachers) is the largest of its kind in the United Kingdom, and is unique.[1] When we began the work few recent studies were in existence that had attempted to identify the key components of effective school leadership through the eyes of those who experience and witness it, while also relating analyses of multi-perspective grounded data to existing theoretical and empirical literature on leadership. Thus, while the number of schools studied for the purposes of this research was twelve, the number of interviews on which the original analysis was based exceeded two hundred, and the number of interviewees was approximately double this number.

The book is divided into eight chapters. Chapter 1, 'The changing face of headship', begins by providing a brief history of the social, economic and policy contexts which have shaped the culture of school leaders' work. It then critically reviews theories of leadership in the international research literature, focusing particularly upon those which apply to leading schools in changing times. It thus provides a background for the research upon which the book is based. Chapter 2, 'Studying leadership in schools from multiple perspectives' presents the aims of the original research study and gives an account of the criteria and means by which the 12 case study schools and their headteachers were selected. It explains the multiple perspectives approach utilized and how data was collected. It also provides an explanation of the process of thematic induction by which the field data were analysed in order to identify the characteristics and behaviours associated with effective leadership in schools and how the constructs of tensions and dilemmas were used to gain new insights, not just into the nature of that leadership, but into headteachers' experience of leadership.

The next four chapters provide different perspectives of effective leadership. Chapter 3, 'The headteachers', provides the perspectives of headteachers themselves. They talk frankly about their hopes and fears as managers and leaders and the benefits and costs of their work to their lives. It is a chapter which reveals the strong presence of the personal within the professional, the keen sense of equity and social justice which heads feel for the education of all their students. The deep care which they demonstrate for all their staff through cultures of collegiality is combined with a strong drive to high standards of achievement and behaviour and their continuing reflection in, on and about the contexts in which these are located. Crucially, it reveals that each has a core set of values which drives the ways in which they react and respond to external and internal change demands. Chapter 4, 'The deputies and teachers', outlines the perspectives of deputy heads and teachers upon effective leadership. Within this chapter deputies and teachers offer their views on the leadership style of the headteacher and evaluate the head's approach to managing the school. Given the increasing research evidence underlining the importance of devolved leadership, the chapter provides an insight into current practice in schools. It explores the degree of consensus concerning effective leadership and illustrates the importance of context in determining leadership behaviour. The chapter also reinforces the centrality of personal values in guiding and shaping effective leadership in practice.

Chapter 5, 'The perspectives of governors, parents and support staff', examines these various perspectives in some depth. From the data it became clear that parents and governors enjoyed a close relationship with their respective schools, and had a clear understanding of the personality and work of their headteachers. They admired the personal values and beliefs which contributed to their set of core values, in particular their enthusiasm, commitment, hard work, honesty, integrity, support for others and a recognition of the worth of individuals. Their responses also showed their recognition of the complexity and demands of the

headteacher's role. The views of support staff were firmly grounded
in the employer–employee relationship. Their headteachers made
them feel valued and respected as important members of the
school team. The informality and intimacy of many of the relationships inspired a sense of loyalty far in excess of that demanded
by their contractual duties. Chapter 6, 'The students' perspectives', explores the perspectives on leadership offered by students,
ranging in age from 7 to 18 years. From the data it was clear
that students' perceptions were derived very much from observation of their headteachers performing in a wide variety of
settings and personal contact. Students, like other groups in the
school community, recognized that their heads had good interpersonal skills and that they held a set of core values which
underpinned their views on student achievement and welfare.
They were also aware of the tensions which applying these core
values could often create within the school community.

Chapter 7, 'School leadership: tensions and dilemmas', focuses
attention back on the headteachers' experience of leadership. It
explores the parameters of leadership by considering the tensions
and dilemmas the headteachers faced. Bringing tensions and
dilemmas together encapsulates the immediacy of leadership,
reveals the centrality of personal values and highlights the stresses
of leading schools in challenging circumstances. Chapter 8, 'Post-
transformational leadership', provides an overview and analysis
of the findings presented in the previous chapters. It begins
by reviewing the relationship between leadership and school
improvement and reinforces the importance of leadership in the
pursuit of school-level change. It then considers the findings
from the original study in the context of a range of theoretical
frameworks present in the leadership literature. In particular,
analytical frameworks derived from work by Bolman and Deal
(1984), Patterson *et al.* (1997), MacBeath (1998) and Leithwood
et al. (1999) provide the basis for reviewing the study's empirical
evidence and findings. These critical analyses lead into a general
consideration of the appropriateness of existing leadership theory
to represent and explain fully current effective leadership practice. The chapter argues that a new form of leadership theory is
required that is values-led and contingency-based. It proposes a
post-transformational theory of leadership that encompasses and
reflects the complexity of leadership behaviour in the changing
times of the late twentieth and early twenty-first centuries. The

findings suggest that reliance upon rational, managerialist theory as the basis for training provision is both limiting and inappropriate, and that a *values-led contingency model of school leadership* needs to be reflected in professional development opportunities for aspirant and serving headteachers. Finally, the chapter looks towards the future and suggests that both policy makers and practitioners need to recognize the importance of values and vision in shaping effective leadership practice in high-reliability learning communities.

We believe that by telling the leadership stories through a mix of participants' accounts, framed by analytical constructs which emerged as we processed the incoming information, and from a critical overview of appropriate international literatures, the book provides an authentic account of the complexity of effective leadership in changing times. There are too many texts which do not give value to the words and experiences of those closest to the action, preferring instead to explore distant theoretical labyrinths. Leadership of schools in changing times is fraught with opportunities and challenges. Leaders are expected to manage competing interests, to create conditions which form the foundation for lifelong learning, and to raise achievement levels of the motivated, the unmotivated and those between. Some do this very successfully, others do not. It is our hope that presenting the stories of those who do will encourage a greater understanding and appreciation of their work, its costs and benefits, and that it will influence in some small way those policy makers, trainers and educators who are dedicated to raising standards in all schools.

Note

1. A copy of the report, *Effective Headteachers*, may be obtained from National Association of Head Teachers, 1 Heath Square, Boltro Road, Haywards Heath, West Sussex, RH16 1BL.

1

THE CHANGING FACE OF HEADSHIP

The challenges posed by the changing demands made upon schools in the past 20 years have exercised the minds of many writers on educational leadership in a number of countries because, while it is broadly agreed that the quality of teaching strongly influences levels of pupil motivation and achievement, it has been consistently argued that the quality of headship matters in determining the motivation of teachers and the quality of teaching which takes place in the classroom (Fullan 1992a, b; Eraut 1994; Hargreaves 1994; Ofsted 1995; Sammons *et al.* 1995; Day *et al.* 1998). In recent years, the government in England seems to have recognized this, though belatedly and against a backdrop of falling levels of recruitment for headships, in the increased attention being given to headship training and education. A School Management Task Force was set up in January 1989 to facilitate school-based management training (DES 1990). The training requirements of heads were further researched six years later (Ofsted *et al.* 1995). The HEADLAMP project was then launched for those in their first two years of headship, followed by a mandatory National Professional Qualification for aspirant heads (NPQH). Training for headship continues to have a rising profile (DfEE 1997; Labour Party 1997). National standards for headteachers have recently been set out in a document which effectively provides a set of strategies by which heads can accommodate within their schools the reform agenda of the past ten years (Teacher Training Agency 1997). In 1998 the first national leadership programme for serving headteachers (LPSH) was launched, followed by the establishment in 2000 of a National College for School Leadership. While these initiatives are to be welcomed, it must not be forgotten that they are located in the context of considerable changes in how education is regarded, what its purposes and content should be, and how its processes and outcomes might be assessed. These changes have considerable implications for relationships between heads and teachers.

A brief historical perspective

I set out to explore the swamp of literature on leadership. It goes on and on and ranges from the sublime to the ridiculous with little in between. Taken as a whole it is a shambles, a mess full of philosophical confusion . . . It is full of word magic of the worst kind . . .

(Hodgkinson, cited in Ribbins 1993: 21)

Reasons for the philosophical confusion highlighted above are not hard to find. The field is still a comparatively new one. Writers on educational management and leadership are still exploring recently charted territory. Prior to 1988, there was no apparent imperative for schools to show an interest in educational management. Few headteachers in the state system had direct control of any significant financial resources to manage in their schools, with only capitation consistently being devolved by LEAs. There was no agreed or imposed national consensus on the aims and objectives of education before the National Curriculum, so there existed no imperative at school level to set up appropriate planning and assessment mechanisms. Interest in educational management, therefore, tended to be limited to the role of the headteacher in motivating staff to achieve local aims and objectives, invariably set by the heads themselves. However, the then Prime Minister Callaghan's speech at Ruskin College in 1976, when he launched a nationwide debate on priorities for the state education system, effectively triggered the growth of centralist, policy-driven intervention into the 'secret-garden' of education.

Educational writers became increasingly interested in the management of what was happening in schools. More than 20
years ago, the collection of essays, edited by Peters, on the role
of the head (Peters 1976) highlighted the need for heads to shift
from their traditional autonomous, paternalistic positions (see
Barrow 1976; Bernbaum 1976; Colegate 1976) to one of increasing accountability to groups both inside and outside their schools
(Coulson 1976). Prior to this, the writing on educational management was coloured by the massive body of literature on industrial management which, until comparatively recently, has largely
been based upon three models. The model of scientific (or
rational–economic) management (Taylor 1911) presented the
work process as a set of discrete and prescribed activities undertaken by individuals who had been rigorously trained in the
process. It was a model characterized by the close supervision of
workers, of regular quality checks of the work done, and a tight
control and measurement of inputs into the process. Targets
were set to increase production. Levels of pay reflected levels
of production, and were seen as the main motivating force for
workers. There are parallels between this and the current reform
agenda in England. This model, however, held little interest for
pre-Local Management of Schools (LMS) writers on educational
management; for the idea of prescription in education ran counter
to the perceived professional autonomy of the teacher. Then
there were no agreed sets of discrete activities to follow, no
tradition of close supervision of teacher activities, and the budgetary information for tight financial checks was not present at
school level. The model, in short, was alien to the perception of
what was happening in most schools.

Even then, however, so-called scientific management had been
criticized on two fronts by other writers on industrial management. What has been called the psycho-sociological or human
relations school (Pollard 1978; Vroom and Deci 1989) had recognized that employees did not work in isolation, but that they
interrelated with fellow workers, with supervisory staff, with
management and with the technology with which they worked.
Hence for these writers human resource management was an
essential element of industrial management. This model of individual and group interaction, and its emphasis upon motivation,
matched more closely the needs arising from what was perceived
to be taking place in schools.

It could be argued that this human relations model might provide a necessary counterbalance to the current rational models of management which have dominated leadership in schools since the late 1980s. Indeed, in the period of growing public interest in the 1970s and calls for increased accountability of the public services, and education in particular, throughout the 1980s, some writers on educational management sought to develop a third model by combining elements of human relations and social systems approaches.

In England, the 1988 Education Reform Act fundamentally changed the locus of policy making in education. Prior to the introduction of LMS and the imposition of a National Curriculum, councillors and education officers at shire and town halls had controlled the allocation of budgets to schools and, alongside this, had exerted a major influence on the formulation and implementation of local educational policy. This system fell into disrepute for a number of reasons. First, government, after a recession triggered by the oil crisis in the mid-1970s, wanted to exercise greater control over all sectors of public expenditure. Second, doubts were raised about the consistency and quality of education in relation to the social and economic needs of a nation which needed to increase its ability to compete in ever more competitive world markets. The notions of a national set of student learning entitlements and more public answerability of schools for student achievements grew. Third, the shift in industry and the public sector towards cash-limited budgeting in the 1980s (Sizer 1989) brought with it the need to set priorities against externally determined targets. This limited the number of activities which could be undertaken by institutions.

With headteachers having to deal increasingly with various interest groups within the community, a number of writers began to address the role of headteacher within the new overtly political context of imposed change. In England, Heller's psychological study of heads created typologies of leadership based upon approaches to change. Extrovert heads, he suggested, reverted to autocratic methods of management where they encountered resistance, and to a charismatic style of leadership where resistance was minimal. Introvert heads retreated in the face of resistance, and where there was co-operation they created bureaucratic structures within the school to implement change slowly (Heller 1985).

Bush's work also related to the head's response to the prevailing micro-political system predominating in schools. He characterized as 'formal' a management system where the head set the institutional goals, and where a hierarchy enforced rules in pursuit of these goals. A 'democratic' system operated where goals were negotiated, where the head was an equal partner with other staff in decision making and where organizations outside the school could negotiate their own involvement in corporate goal setting. In a 'political' system the dominant coalitions within the school dictated the goals. Meetings were areas for conflict, with the head as participant or mediator (Bush 1986).

In the 1980s, also, considerable attention was given to models of response to what Bolam had called the 'user system' in schools, both to managerial style (Hoyle 1986; Blase 1989) and to innovation (Bolam 1975; Thomas 1987). A number of writers lamented the potential for deprofessionalization of the teacher in this new context of increased managerialism (Taylor 1976; Bottery 1988, 1992; Day *et al.* 1993). With some notable exceptions (e.g. Nias *et al.* 1989; Wallace 1991; MacBeath 1998), school-based empirical studies, particularly of relations with external systems such as parents and governors, were, and still are, less in evidence. Changes in the power relationships within the system of school governance, however, make such studies crucial to an understanding of the changing contexts of school leadership and management (Sarason 1990) and efforts to improve them which are based on reality rather than well-intentioned rhetoric.

The current context

A process of ideological transformation is occurring in contemporary English society in which education is regarded as a commodity; the schools as a value-adding production unit; the headteacher as chief executive and managing director; the parents as consumers; and the ultimate aim of the whole enterprise to achieve a maximum value-added product which keeps the school as near to the top of the league table of success as possible . . . Contemporary headteachers are therefore expected to 'market the school', 'deliver the curriculum', and to 'satisfy the customers'.

(Grace 1995: 21)

The document which represented the sea change in government policy and heralded the fundamental shift in school governance which was to lead to radical changes in headteachers' roles in schools was the Coopers and Lybrand report to the then Department of Education and Science (DES) on LMS, published in 1988. It looked at a number of pilot projects, and posited the enhancement of the planning process at school level as the main justification for introducing LMS nationally. The report also gave an indicator of the imminent changes in the role of heads:

> The change at school level is from administration (of centrally determined programmes) to management (of local resources). What is required is a fundamental change in the philosophy of the organisation of education. Thus the changes required in the culture and in the management processes are much wider than purely financial and should be recognised as such . . . We therefore propose that the concept is referred to by the more accurate term: 'Local Management of Schools'.
>
> (Coopers and Lybrand 1988: paragraphs 1.12, 1.13)

The range of responses by headteachers to the differing management requirements since 1988 has been located between the extreme poles of the scientific/rational–economic and systems models of management. A rational–economic approach would see schools assessing what is necessary in resource terms to operate effectively, then match that assessment to the resources available (Davies 1989). Partly in response to this, it has been suggested that the 'objectification' of the resource management task as implied in the rational–economic model ignores the subjective experience of groups, or 'actors', within the school, and that this must be considered if school planning is to be effective (Strain 1990). The systems model would see typically historical patterns of funding adopted, and some of the goals of different groupings within the school community satisfied, sometimes at the expense of the organizational goals of the school. For example, teachers might resist the suggested redundancy of a colleague in an overstaffed but under-equipped school. Between these two extremes of complete internal adjustment (deference) and strategic redefinition (resistance) lies a strategy adopted by most schools, that of strategic compliance (Riseborough 1993).

What such a compliance or accommodation has meant in terms of changes in workload for heads has attracted much interest. Early critics of LMS pointed to the increased administrative workload (Heywood 1986; Tagg 1986; Harrison 1987; Pipes 1988; Lamb 1990). Although it has been suggested subsequently that a concentration on administration is largely a matter of personal choice for heads (Ribbins 1996) there is no doubt that the bureaucratic and person management demands upon them have increased as root and branch reforms have been accompanied by new responsibilities for accounting and reporting. This perceived shift, along with the introduction of the National Curriculum, has resulted in a sense for some heads that their functions as pedagogic role models and curriculum leaders in their schools have diminished (Mortimore and Mortimore 1991; Southworth 1995). This in turn can potentially cause them to be professionally isolated from the rest of their staff (Dennison 1988; Nightingale 1988). Some writers have seen this shift in activity, either voluntary or involuntary, to issues of staffing, maintenance and fund raising (see Saunders 1987; Fidler and Bowles 1989; Gold 1990; Wilkinson 1990) as requiring a change in the qualities required by headteachers, particularly in the primary sector: 'The self-concept of the . . . head has had to shift from that of educational-leader/paternalist/community-servant to that of manager/salesperson of an educational commodity' (Menter *et al.* 1995).

Effective headship, it seems, has become characterized by personal assertiveness, firm leadership, entrepreneurship and strong managerial control in the workplace (Evetts 1993, 1994). The collaborative collegiality which prevailed in pre-1988 decision-making processes in schools has been replaced by 'responsible autonomy' in a context of 'managed participation' through teacher compliance to internalized aims and controls (Menter *et al.* 1995). Others have suggested a similar approach, where heads focus activity in the school upon maximizing learning outcomes and student achievement (Hopkins *et al.* 1994; Clarke 1995; Hallinger and Heck 1996). In England, Southworth has outlined the dilemma of primary heads having to relinquish the reins of curriculum leadership, while needing to pay even more attention, since the advent of Ofsted, to the quality of teaching and learning in their classrooms (Southworth 1995, 1996).

It would be a mistake to regard reforms in school governance as applying only to England. They are part of an international trend towards a perception by governments, concerned as they are with increased economic competitiveness and the fragmentation of values in society, that schools are not doing enough to raise student achievement and awareness of the responsibility of citizenship. In Canada, for example, Fullan has described a climate of 'dependency' where schools are liable to use up all their collective energies in accommodating and implementing governments' reform agendas at the expense of their own (Fullan 1998). He outlines a ten-point programme to develop the schools' own agenda by empowering teachers, by building alliances within the educational community and by taking calculated risks in promoting the school's vision.

Leadership imperatives, new directions

Education and schooling, then, have become subject to an ongoing plethora of imposed curriculum and management innovations and increasing quality control, and are being judged more and more on output measures. These externally generated initiatives have fundamentally challenged priorities within some schools:

> The moral economy of schooling is in danger of losing other commitments (where they existed) to community, collegiality, social justice and the public good. None of these considerations is thought to be measurably productive of success in the educational market place as currently constituted. Headteachers who take such values seriously as part of the educational process seem likely to face much sharper dilemmas in trying to resolve the contradictions.
>
> (Grace 1995: 21)

Heads and teachers must now work with a number of reform paradoxes:

- an apparent increase in independence in the management of schools alongside increasing dependence upon curriculum, monitoring, assessment and inspection frameworks imposed by government;
- a performance and results orientation which has the potential to create divisiveness;

- new forms of accountability which are intended to enhance effectiveness, but which simultaneously increase workload and bureaucracy;
- new imposed curriculum certainties which reduce teachers' abilities to recognize and act upon differentiated student need;
- increased attention to cognitive challenge which reduces attention to emotional need.

In recent years a voluminous literature on leadership, effective schools and school improvement has sprung up which offers a bewildering array of theories, models, principles and strategies for aspiring and serving headteachers. Although a variety of conceptual models of leadership have been generated over the past fifteen years, two major approaches have predominated. The most influential leadership concepts in current times are those of James McGregor Burns who, more than 20 years ago, distinguished between 'transactional' and 'transformative' leadership.

Transactional leadership is based on the exchange relationships between leader and follower. Leithwood (1992) suggests that transactional leadership is based on an exchange of services for various kinds of rewards that the leader controls. The role of the transactional leader, therefore, is to focus upon the purposes of the organization and to assist people to recognize what needs to be done in order to reach a desired outcome. This approach to leadership places its faith in procedures and hard data to inform decision making. It is technically driven and geared towards improving organizations through improving systems.

Transactional leadership, as a form of scientific managerialism, is premised upon a number of core assumptions. First, that there are rewards within the system. Second, that the leader has control over the rewards. Third, that the followers recognize and desire those rewards. In the current context of schooling, the application of this model is limited by the absence of clear tangible rewards within the system. However, with the future implementation of performance-related pay (*Times Educational Supplement,* 11 June 1999) the three assumptions highlighted above may be more readily secured.

In itself, however, even in the current context, transactional management is insufficient to stimulate improvement. Burns suggests that to achieve this requires transformative leadership – a process within which 'leaders and followers raise one another to higher levels of morality and motivation' (Burns 1978: 20). Transformational leaders not only manage structure but they purposefully impact upon the culture in order to change it. Burns (1978) describes transformational leadership as being concerned with exploring conventional relationships and organizational understandings through involvement and participation.

Twenty-one years later, Ken Leithwood, one of the world's foremost researchers on school leadership, and his colleagues, in an authoritative and scholarly work on leadership for changing times, provide evidence of the enduring power of this concept for schools in times of change. However, they warn against falsely dichotemizing transformational and transactional forms, agreeing with Bass and Avolio (1993) that the latter needs to build upon the former.

They propose that the seven dimensions of transformational leadership in schools identified earlier (Leithwood 1994) may now be organized into different categories:

- setting directions (includes vision building, goal consensus and the development of high-performance expectations);
- developing people (includes the provision of individualized support, intellectual stimulation and the modelling of values and practices important to the mission of the school);
- organizing (culture building in which colleagues are motiv-ated by moral imperatives and structuring, fostering shared decision-making processes and problem-solving capacities);
- building relationships with the school community.

(Leithwood *et al.* 1999: 39)

The inclusion of the school–community factor moves their work beyond previous notions of transformational leadership, recog-nizing that this forms a core part of effective leadership. Addition-ally, they highlight the importance in high-reliability learning communities of leaders who are able to maintain their own 'emotional balance', identify and communicate their values and demonstrate care and respect for others.

In recent empirical research in primary (elementary) schools in England, Southworth and his colleagues were able to confirm that the main concerns of heads relate still to the need to build trust and self-confidence, and to maintain staff morale, purpose and unity (Southworth *et al.* 1998). Effective leadership today, then, seems to demand a clear set of core values and the ability to exercise a balance in practice between a sense of vision, high-achievement expectations and a commitment to capacity building among staff.

Recently, leadership studies have focused upon values – the 'moral purposes' and moral craft of leadership (Tom 1984; Sergiovanni 1992); the roles of leaders in creating a 'community of learners' (Barth 1990a; Senge 1990); and the capacities of leaders to 'make a difference' through their ability to 'transform' (Sergiovanni 1995) or 'liberate' (Tampoe 1998) rather than simply 'transact'. Sergiovanni suggests that when transformative leadership is practised successfully, 'purposes which may have initially seemed to be separate, become fused' (Sergiovanni 1995: 119). The articulation, development and implementation of 'vision' is particularly crucial in such capacity building:

> ... developing the necessary self-confidence to withstand the stresses and strains encountered when external and internal priorities conflict is essential for the well-being of a modern principal. Refining, understanding and confirming the educational values that lie at the heart of consistent decision-making are important components of principals' professional learning. A set of professional values is necessary if principals are to mediate productive settlements in contradictory situations ...
>
> (Dempster and Logan, in MacBeath 1998: 96)

However:

> It is one thing for a leader to have the vision: it is quite another for that vision to guide the behaviour of an entire organisation. Leaders in successful quality settings have been able to conceptualise the theory in ways that translate into practice, steer the change process, and guide their people in determining not only how to perform their jobs, but even more importantly, what those jobs should be.
>
> (Siegel and Byrne 1994: 52)

Headteachers who practise effective leadership in the competing value frameworks of the post-modern age will engage in bartering, building, bonding and binding simultaneously according to circumstance. Their focus will always be upon the person and the task and the broader stakeholder contexts. They will be leaders and managers who pay close attention also to building learning and achievement cultures in their schools and communities. This is not as straightforward as it may appear at first sight, for staff-rooms, like classrooms, are complex, micropolitical environments.

In England, Ball (1987), Burgess (1988) and Bowe and Ball (1992) have pointed to the widening role gap between teachers and headteachers as structural reform has increased the management functions of heads, moving them towards a 'chief executive' role (Hughes 1985; Grace 1995) and giving less time for them to perform their 'leading professional' roles (Pollard *et al.* 1994). Exceptions to this are to be found mainly in primary schools (Acker 1990; Woods 1993).

Leadership and management

As a result of the impact of reform on schools it has been necessary to define more clearly two essential and complementary functions of headteachers – those which relate to management and those which relate to leadership. It has been argued by some, for example, that 'good management controls complexity; effective leadership produces useful change' (Kotter 1990); and others have summarized the key orientations of the former, which is about control, and the latter, which is about 'liberation' (Tampoe 1998):

LEADING is concerned with:	MANAGING is concerned with:
• vision	• implementation
• strategic issues	• operational issues
• transformation	• transaction
• ends	• means
• people	• systems
• doing the right things	• doing things right

(West-Burnham 1997)

Brian Caldwell, so long at the heart of the establishment and development of the self-managing school movement in Australia (Caldwell and Spinks 1992, 1998) elaborates on the challenges for principals by underlining the complexities of their roles. He proposes that school reform is proceeding on three tracks:

Track 1:   Self-managing schools in the public sector.
Track 2:   Unrelenting focus on restructuring learning and
           teaching.
Track 3:   Schooling for the knowledge society.

(Caldwell 1999)

Citing meta-analysis of 70 evaluations of the impact of self-managing schools (Summers and Johnson 1996) he notes that in Track 1, the focus was on organizational processes, with virtually no attention to how process changes may affect student performance. The need to move to Track 2 is justified by this and other research findings in America and Europe (OECD 1994; Smith *et al.* 1996; Bullock and Thomas 1997). In short, 'to improve student learning, the content and instruction delivered to students must change as well as the organizational structure of the school. They complement each other' (Smith *et al.* 1996: 21). Caldwell's vision of Track 3 includes connectedness in the curriculum; cyber policy; access and equity; virtual schools; school fabric; globalization; workplace transformation; and professionalism; and great teaching and is not unlike that of David Hargreaves (Hargreaves 1997). The leadership and management of each of these 'tracks', and movement between them, implies the need for highly knowledgeable and skilled teachers and school leaders who are confident in their leadership purposes, personal integrity and professional knowledge, and competent in their practices. In this context, Caldwell suggests five dimensions of transformational leadership:

- *cultural leadership,* referring to a culture of excellence underpinned by the values of quality, effectiveness, equity, efficiency and empowerment, and effecting a shift from a culture of dependence in a centralized system to a culture of self-management;
- *strategic leadership,* referring to a capacity to understand emerging trends in society at large and in schools generally, discerning their likely and preferred impact on their school; working with others to develop a capacity for state-of-the-art learning;
- *educational leadership,* referring to the building of capacity among teachers, parents and students by 'nurturing a learning community';

- *responsive leadership*, effectively, 'coming to terms with accountability' by recognizing the right of different individuals and institutions to know how well the school is doing;
- *strategic management*, which involved emergent strategy, strategic planning, entrepreneurship and strategic intent.

(Caldwell 1999: 259)

This fifth dimension is drawn from the work of Boisot (1995), and it is strategic intent, 'the distinguishing mark of the learning organisation and, by implication, an essential component of its repertoire' (Boisot 1995: 41), which, with educational leadership, is most applicable to the theme of this book:

Strategic intent describes a process of coping with turbulence through a direct, intuitive understanding. A turbulent environment cannot be tamed by rational analysis alone so that conventional strategic planning is deemed to be of little use. Yet it does not follow that [a school's] adaptive response must be left to a random distribution of lone individuals acting opportunistically and often in isolation as in a regime of entrepreneurship. Strategic intent relies on an intuitively formed pattern or gestalt – some would call it vision – to give it unity and coherence.

(Adapted from Boisot 1995: 36, cited in Caldwell 1997)

Leadership and culture

Culture and leadership are two sides of the same coin in that leaders first create cultures when they create groups and organisations. Once cultures exist, they determine the criteria for leadership and thus determine who will or will not be a leader. But if cultures become dysfunctional, it is the unique function of leadership to perceive the functional and dysfunctional elements of the existing culture and to manage cultural evolution and change in such a way that the group can survive in a changing environment.

(Schein 1988: 15)

The importance of headteachers in the creation, management and leadership of culture in schools is well documented (Rutter *et al.* 1979; Ball 1987; Southworth 1993; Hargreaves 1994), as is their role in school effectiveness and improvement (Reynolds 1991; Mortimore *et al.* 1994; Troman 1996). In England, Mortimore *et al.* (1988) found 'purposeful leadership of staff' to be a characteristic of successful schools; and in Canada, Leithwood and Janzti (1990) concluded that principals who 'were effective at transforming the culture of the school toward a stronger improvement orientation' (Fullan 1992b) used six strategies. They:

1. strengthened the school's culture;
2. used a variety of bureaucratic mechanisms to stimulate and reinforce cultural change;
3. fostered staff development;
4. engaged in direct and frequent communication about cultural norms, values and belief;
5. shared power and responsibility with others;
6. used symbols to express cultural values.

   (Leithwood and Jantzi, cited in Fullan 1992a: 86)

There is no doubt that teachers themselves prefer principals who are honest, communicative, participatory, collegial, informal, supportive and demanding and reasonable in their expectations with a clear vision for the school – principals who work 'with' rather than 'through' (Nias *et al.* 1989; Rosenholtz 1989). However,

Collaborative forms of teacher development may in many instances not be empowering teachers towards greater professional independence at all, but incorporating them and their loyalties within processes and structures bureaucratically determined elsewhere.

   (Hargreaves and Dawe 1990: 228)

Cultures are moving mosaics of beliefs, values, understandings, attitudes, norms, symbols, rituals and ceremonies, preferred behaviours, styles and stances and power structures (Nias *et al.* 1989). Relationships between the various parts will not be static. While they represent collective and individual histories, they are located in the present and for the future. Since they represent, in simplest terms, 'the way we do things and relate to each other around here' (Deal and Kennedy 1984), each teacher, student, parent and governor will affect the *cultural equilibrium* of the school as indeed will external intervention.

While it is possible to identify collective cultures in many primary schools (Nias *et al.* 1989), this is not always appropriate for larger primary or secondary schools; for, while school mission statements and developmental plans may abound, they may be an agglomeration of, or even compromise between, different departmental subcultures, competing 'interest groups' and the influence of powerful individuals (Hargreaves 1994; Talbert and McLaughlin 1994). In 'balkanised', 'individualism' and 'comfortably collaborative' cultures (Hargreaves 1994), it is likely that development will be evolutionary to the point that it becomes culturally extinct without external intervention. Cultures of contrived collegiality, if a 'bridging' process towards more collaborative cultures, provide added opportunities for development. In the moving mosaic and collaborative culture, where critical reflection and experimentation are the norm, development will be continual. So, at any given time there are likely to be differences both within and between schools in terms of their phase of development. In America, for example, Rosenholtz (1989), in a study of 78 elementary schools, found that those which were 'moving', in which teachers learned from one another and from outside, and in which improvements in teaching were seen as a collective responsibility and enterprise, were more effective than schools which were 'stuck'.

Leadership and continuing professional development

Effective responses to the challenges of contemporary classrooms require a spirited, reflective professional community of teachers – a workplace setting that allows examination of assumptions about practice, focuses collective expertise on solutions based on classroom realities, and supports efforts to change and grow professionally. Strong professional communities allow the expression of new ideas and innovations in terms of specific curricula and student characteristics. Energetic professional communities at the school or department level actually generate motivation to roll up one's sleeves and endeavour to meet the unfamiliar and often difficult needs of contemporary students . . .

(McLaughlin 1993: 98)

As teaching and learning environments have changed in response to new challenges, so the importance of teachers' continuing professional development has been recognized as being a crucial element in effective schools. In America, Barth has called upon heads to become 'head learners' in their schools (Barth 1990a, b, 1996), creating a community of curriculum leaders, maintaining high expectations of staff and students and exercising authority through quality control (see also McNally and Patching 1994; Ainscow and Southworth 1995; Southworth 1995). An important element in the exercise of authority is visibility around the school (Southworth 1990; Riley and Mahony 1995). Such a leadership style has impacted upon teacher reflection, has facilitated staff development and has enhanced feelings of professional worth (Hayes and Ross 1989; Mapstone 1990; Moisan 1990; Louis *et al.* 1994).

Leithwood *et al.* at OISE's (the Ontario Institute for Studies in Education) Centre for Leadership Development provide insights into 'how to influence people to work willingly for group goals':

> The leadership problem . . . has three parts: developing a widely shared, defensible vision; in the short run, directly assisting members of the school community to overcome obstacles they encounter in striving for the vision; and, in the long run, increasing the capacity of members of the school community to overcome subsequent obstacles more successfully and with greater ease.
>
> (Leithwood *et al.* 1992: 8)

Effective leaders aim to build 'learning enriched' schools for staff as well as pupils through participative leadership which is

> . . . fuelled by a vision of possibilities. Their vision leads to a sense of the drama being played out everyday in the school. It is a drama of becoming a people, learning how to participate, how to negotiate, how to forgive, how to celebrate heroic ideals . . .
>
> (Starratt 1993: 57)

Hallinger and Murphy (1985) distinguish between cognitive goals (specific statements about desired results) and cathartic goals which concern the mission of the school and describe the organization's core or primary values. These non-rational goals act as a source of identification and motivation for staff, giving meaning to their work, binding them to the organization (Staessens and Vandenburghe 1994). Thus, a vital function of leaders is to manage both rational and non-rational goals in their daily interactions with colleagues.

Howard Gardner has identified six features of successful leaders and the implications of these for school leaders, which link directly into their role as lead learners, leading values:

Features of successful leaders	Implications for school leaders
1. Central story or message	Knowledge of pedagogy, school and community they serve
2. Acute awareness of audience	Knowledge of and ability to communicate with all stakeholders
3. Require an institutional or organisational basis	Pay attention to detail including maintenance and development
4. Live her/his story	Act in a way which accords with espoused values
5. Lead in both direct and indirect ways	Able to take up front role, team role, observer role and delegate with confidence
6. Adapt to change and new knowledge	Able to take on the role of lead learner

(Gardner 1995)

The literature suggests that ongoing success, then, in self-managing schools will depend upon the commitment and abilities of head-teachers to promote professional development awareness cultures in their schools. Teachers who are provided regularly and appropriately with opportunities for self-renewal of vision and purpose, and who are helped to acquire new habits and review existing habits of thought, disposition and practice, will, it seems, develop their capacity to contribute to the task of enhancing the quality of students' learning opportunities and to the development of their colleagues' thinking and practices (Rudduck 1991: 138).

Conclusion

The studies of effective leadership and management cited in this chapter and other recent studies of highly effective business leaders and headteachers in England and elsewhere confirm that they are person-centred and strongly driven by sets of personal values (religious, spiritual, humanistic) which create a 'passionate conviction' to build, implement and continually monitor a vision for excellence in learning and achievement by means of feedback from stakeholders inside and outside the school; that skills and behaviours of effective leaders are driven by beliefs and trust in self and others; and that effective leaders recognize and are skilled in managing tensions and dilemmas within a framework of competing values. The findings reported in this study confirm much of this research, but go beyond them, revealing a much more complex picture of leadership in action, recognizing that leadership is as much about developing the self alongside high levels of emotional commitment as it is about capacity building in others; and that effective leadership requires an intelligent head with an intelligent heart.

2

STUDYING LEADERSHIP
IN SCHOOLS FROM
MULTIPLE PERSPECTIVES

Research goals

The primary aim of the research was to contribute to the knowledge and understanding of contemporary leadership in schools through a synthesis of theoretical perspectives derived from the literature and new evidence obtained by means of empirical enquiry. The main objectives of the project, therefore, were to:

- collect data in schools from a multiplicity of perspectives including those of headteachers, deputy headteachers, governors, parents, students, support staff and teachers;
- compare effective leadership in contexts ranging from small rural primary schools to large urban secondary schools;
- identify the personal qualities and professional competencies which are generic to effective leadership in schools;
- re-examine existing theoretical perspectives on school leadership through insights derived from new empirical research;
- contribute to the wider educational debate on the relationship between leadership and school effectiveness and improvement.

It was concluded that these goals could not be achieved through a research design based on either a large-scale quantitative survey or an ethnographic study of a single school. It was decided, therefore, to adopt a methodological approach which involved qualitative fieldwork concentrated into a period of three days in each of 12 carefully chosen case study schools.

Selecting the case study schools

The choice of research methods was based on the assumption that the concept of 'effectiveness' when applied to the leadership provided by headteachers is both a contextualized and relational construct, and as such it would have to be investigated by reference to multiple perspectives within schools. A sample of schools was then selected which provided a wide range of contexts and leadership challenges. This was done by means of a matrix which was constructed around three dimensions which would allow for theory-generating case studies (Yin 1989) to be chosen on the basis of representing 'extreme cases' (Walker 1989) or 'maximum variation sampling' (Maykut and Morehouse 1994). These dimensions were:

- schools of different sizes operating within different phases of education (i.e. the early years of primary schooling through to upper secondary and including special schools);
- schools located within a range of economic and socio-cultural settings (i.e. including rural, suburban and inner-urban schools as well as those with mixed catchment areas);
- schools in which headteachers who were widely acknowledged as being 'effective' leaders had spent different amounts of time (i.e. ranging from relatively new to well-established headteachers with many years of experience).

Given the goals of the research, the most critical and problematic of these dimensions concerned the selection of schools in which the headteacher met the criterion of providing 'effective' leadership. In this respect the research team was in the paradoxical situation of having to define what it meant by 'effective' in order to select the schools in which it would then begin to investigate the personal qualities and professional competencies generic to 'effective leadership'. The dilemma was resolved by the adoption of a working definition which enabled schools to be chosen on the basis of the following criteria:

Table 2.1 Case study schools and their head teachers

School	School status (and type – mixed unless stated)	Pupils numbers on roll (and age range)	Geographical location (and catchment area)	Gender of headteacher (and years of service as a teacher)	Years as headteacher of present school (and number of headships)
S1	Maintained (Primary)	416 (4–11)	North-East England (Urban)	30 (Female)	14 (2)
S2	Voluntary Controlled (Secondary Comprehensive)	1739 (11–18)	Greater Manchester (Urban)	37 (Male)	15 (2)
S3	Voluntary Controlled (Primary)	358 (4–11)	Greater Manchester (Inner City)	26 (Male)	8 (2)
S4	Voluntary Aided (Primary)	760 (3–11)	West Midlands Conurbation (Inner City)	31 (Male)	16 (2)
S5	Maintained (Primary)	340 (4–11)	East Anglia (Rural)	23 (Male)	12 (1)
S6	Maintained (Primary)	91 (4–11)	East Anglia (Rural)	26 (Female)	7 (1)
S7	Maintained (Comprehensive Upper)	868 (13–18)	East Anglia (Rural and Urban)	30 (Male)	13 (1)
S8	Maintained (Primary)	630 (4–11)	East Anglia (Urban)	25 (Female)	2 (2)
S9	Maintained (Infant)	116 (3–8)	Greater London (Inner City)	10 (Female)	6 (1)
S10	Maintained (Boys' Residential Special)	62 (11–16)	South (Rural)	9 (Male)	9 (1)
S11	Maintained (Infant and Nursery)	270 (3–7)	East Midlands (Inner City)	30 (Female)	9 (1)
S12	Maintained (Comprehensive)	560 (11–16)	East Midlands (Urban)	22 (Female)	5 (1)

- schools which had received a 'positive' Inspection Report by Ofsted, particularly with regard to the leadership provided by the headteacher;
- schools which, on the basis of 'league tables' of SATs and examination results, could be shown to be performing better than local and national means;
- schools in which their headteachers were widely acknowledged by their professional peers (through the local, regional and national networks of the NAHT) as being 'effective' leaders.

Once potential schools meeting all the above criteria had been identified it was then necessary through a process of negotiation (in which the NAHT acted as an intermediary) for the research team to gain access to schools in which the headteachers were prepared to:

- subject themselves to intensive questioning during three interviews, each lasting for at least an hour;
- give the researchers access to deputy headteachers, governors, parents, students, support staff and teachers in order to conduct one-to-one and group interviews which would focus (perhaps critically) on the leadership which they had experienced;
- organize and manage a programme of interviews and group meetings over a period of three days at a busy time in the school year (February–June).

Information about the 12 case study schools and their headteachers who satisfied the selection criteria and were willing to participate in the research are summarized in Table 2.1.

Research protocol

The first step taken by the project team in the development of its research methodology was the creation of a set of ethical guidelines and an organizational framework for the collection, processing and analysis of data and the publication of the outcomes of the enquiry. The resultant 'research protocol' fulfilled a number of important functions. In particular, it clarified the purposes of the project for the benefit of the case study schools and specified what would be expected of them by the researchers on the occasion of their fieldwork visits. In return the schools were given reassurances about such matters as the storage and retrieval of research data, the negotiation of confidentiality and the preservation of anonymity. The protocol also addressed the question of the reliability of the research by providing a framework aimed at ensuring that all members of the project team adopted a similar approach to the conduct of their field visits to individual case study schools. This protocol was reinforced by the use of research instruments, especially interview schedules, which were common to all of the participating schools.

Adopting a multiple perspectives approach

Given that the leadership provided by headteachers is widely acknowledged to be a crucial variable in determining the effectiveness of schools, it is not surprising that the existing literature is rich in the number of research studies which examine different aspects of the role of the headteacher. However, as Ribbins and Sherratt (1992) pointed out, the majority of these studies consist of:

- surveys which 'seek to say something about the views of heads and draw upon direct quotations from interviews' which the researcher has conducted with headteachers; and
- case studies written by headteachers which draw heavily upon their own experience, and as such are essentially 'autobiographical' in the perspective they provide on leadership in schools.

On the evidence of the literature, therefore, it would appear that previous research has relied too heavily on headteachers themselves as the primary source of data on leadership in schools. However, the evidence is that when researchers do turn their attention to alternative perspectives they prove to be rich sources of data. For example, studies of pupils' views about school (Babad *et al.* 1991; SooHoo 1993; Rudduck *et al.* 1996a; Smees and Thomas 1998) reveal that they 'can be both astute and articulate observers of the school environment' (Smees and Thomas ibid.). The project team concluded that, by failing to draw upon the different 'perspectives' provided by students, teachers and others, previous research has clearly ignored a plethora of evidence about both the 'production' and the 'consumption' of leadership in schools.

The project adopted the view, therefore, that since the workings of the real world (even at the scale of a very small primary
school) can be bewilderingly complex, no single observer, not
even the most perceptive of headteachers, can possibly see or
hear everything and such an observer is condemned to viewing
from a particular perspective or 'angle of observation' (Schatzman
and Strauss 1973). The opinions of any individual, therefore, are
inherently 'biased' by the position from which they have observed
events in what Shimara (1990) has called 'contexts in process'. The
research on which this report is based, therefore, was designed
to capture the 'silent voices' (SooHoo 1993) of authentic sources
of data about leadership in the case study schools on the assumption that new insights would inevitably arise if all too familiar
situations were viewed afresh from 'new angles' (Schatzman and
Strauss 1973; Morgan 1993).

In addition to enabling the project to draw upon hitherto
untapped and highly fruitful sources of evidence, the adoption
of this multiple perspectives approach made it possible to compare data collected from different perspectives and sources for
the purposes of triangulation (Hammersley and Atkinson 1983;
Gill and Johnson 1991).

Collecting the data

The main methods used to collect data in the case study schools
were:

- a short fact-finding questionnaire;
- one-to-one interviews;
- group interviews.

The questionnaire was completed by the headteachers of all the
case study schools. One-to-one interviews, normally taking 45
minutes to an hour to complete, were conducted with headteachers, deputy headteachers, chairs of governors and some
teachers and support staff using pre-prepared interview schedules.
No selection was involved in the case of headteachers, deputies
and chairs of governors and in the case of the small schools in
the sample all staff were interviewed. However, all the other
participants (for both the one-to-one interview and the group
interviews) were nominated by the headteachers. This was judged

to be acceptable on methodological grounds since the team was interested in perspectives on effective leadership.

The headteachers were all interviewed on three separate occasions as follows:

- on the afternoon of the first day to confirm the arrangements for the visit, respond to queries concerning the research methodology, obtain background information on the school and discuss the biographical data which had been provided by the headteacher by means of the questionnaire;
- on the morning of the second day to address the issues identified in the project's protocol and set out in the form of questions in a semi-structured interview schedule;
- on the afternoon of the third day to report back on the organization of the visit, seek clarification of any outstanding issues and to give the headteacher an opportunity, in the light of reflection, to develop or modify answers given to questions in the previous interviews and to give a metaphorical response (see below) to the question of her/his personal approach to leadership.

All the other respondents were interviewed only once. Group interviews were used with some parents and teachers and with all of the students who took part in the research. These group meetings also lasted for 45 minutes to an hour, the discussion being based on the same generic questions as those used in the one-to-one interviews. With the permission of the participants the researchers made use of audio-cassette recorders. Transcriptions were made of the recordings and selected highlights were transferred to memorandum recorders for use as sources of direct quotations. The data collection instruments used in the research were subjected to small-scale piloting prior to their use in the fieldwork phase of the project. During the early stages of the latter, feedback from the first two school visits was used to 'fine-tune' the ways in which the instruments were subsequently used.

In addition to the collection of primary data, documentary evidence was obtained from such secondary sources as school development plans, school prospectuses, Ofsted Inspection Reports, newsletters and examples of media coverage. These sources were used to contextualize the empirical data and as a means of cross-checking their validity and reliability.

Questionnaire

A short questionnaire was used to collect statistical and other factual information about the case study schools, and biographical data on the headteachers. It was sent out to schools and returned in advance of the fieldwork visits in order to provide the project team with background information which it would be useful to have prior to commencing their school-based research. The data obtained by this means were used to compile Table 2.1.

One-to-one interviews

Given the project's commitment to collecting new empirical data from a multiplicity of perspectives from within school organiza-tions, and in so doing seeking to capture the 'authentic voices' of headteachers and other stakeholders, it was inevitable that the field research would centre around some form of interview-ing. The fact that the fieldwork would have to be undertaken by five different researchers working independently, and the large number of interviews which would have to be conducted across twelve case study schools, pointed to the need to make use of common interview schedules in the interests of reliability. In the event it was decided that semi-structured interviews (Drever 1995) based upon a series of open questions would be the most effective means of reconciling the aim of encouraging respondents to talk freely and openly about what they perceived to be signi-ficant with the need, in the interests of comparability, to ensure that topics considered to be crucial to the research were not neglected. The questions and the sequence in which they were organized, therefore, were designed to provide a common agenda for discussions between different respondents and interviewers across the 12 case study schools.

The schedules also provided the interviewer with a set of 'notes for guidance' for the conduct of the interviews. These took the form of a checklist of guidelines and instructions covering such practical matters as the aims and purposes of the interview and its duration, seeking permission to use an audio-cassette recorder, giving reassurances about confidentiality, and how to begin and conclude the meeting. Each of the questions was accompanied by suggested prompts and supplementary questions or 'probes' which an interviewer might use to obtain further details, invite the respondent to elaborate or to seek clarification (Patton 1990). Space was provided beneath each item in the schedules to allow the interviewers to make their field notes. These were used to supplement the evidence provided by the tape recordings and, in the small minority of instances in which permission to record was withheld, as detailed notebooks.

Group interviews

Information was collected from students in all the case study schools by means of small discussion groups (maximum size ten) run as 'focus groups' (Morgan 1988; Krueger 1994) rather than by means of one-to-one interviews. In each case the discussion was started by inviting the students to discuss their own concrete experiences of being a leader (however modest these might have been) and to reflect on those experiences before asking them to discuss leadership in their school, particularly that exercised by the headteacher. In general, they responded positively to the experience, exchanged views in an orderly and disciplined way, developed each other's ideas and were self-confident and articulate. The role adopted by the researcher was that of a 'facilitator' of interaction rather than that of an active 'interrogator'. Consequently, interventions were kept to the minimum and when they were made they were mainly to seek clarification from individuals or to redirect the discussion. A similar format was used in some of the schools with groups of teachers and parents, though in these cases the participants were not asked to discuss their own personal experiences of leadership before being invited to address the substantive issues.

Metaphorical response

All the respondents in the one-to-one interviews and those who participated in focus groups were invited at the end of the discussion to identify a metaphor or metaphors to sum up or 'characterize' the leadership provided by the headteacher of their school. In essence, what they were being asked to do by identifying such metaphors was to 'clarify the meaning of abstract concepts by comparing them to concrete easily understood ones' (Beck and Murphy 1993). Their task, however, was more demanding than that, because what they had to do was link the abstract concept of 'leadership in schools' with a notion which was not only concrete and easy to comprehend, but which was apposite for their particular headteacher. As the examples given in Chapter 6 illustrate, the students in particular proved capable of coping more than adequately with this task – many of their metaphors showing what Fernandez (1986) called 'the profundity of concrete immediacy'.

Analysing the data

It was inevitable that 36 days of qualitative fieldwork in the case study schools which included, e.g., a total of 36 one-to-one interviews of a minimum of one hour's duration with their headteachers would yield a rich abundance of data in the form of field notes, audio-cassette recordings and the researchers' own recollections and impressions of their experiences. The principles and procedures of qualitative research as derived from ethnomethodology and phenomenology (Tesch 1990) were used in the analysis of this plethora of evidence.

Consequently, the analysis of the field evidence was not deferred until the end of the project. It began early and proceeded concurrently with the collection of data in schools so that the two became closely integrated (Glaser and Strauss 1967) to the extent that they began to inform each other (Miles and Huberman 1984). The simultaneous collection and analysis of data was a reflective activity, both individually and for the team as a whole. This process of reflection took a number of forms including periodic meetings of the project team at which progress was reviewed and ideas and opinions were discussed usually as a result of analytical notes (or 'memos') based on the reflections of individuals. These reflective documents and the discussions they prompted furthered the process of analysis by helping the team to move between concrete field data and conceptualization. They also provide an accountable record or 'audit trail' (Lincoln and Guba 1985) which showed that the process of reflection and inductive data analysis not only occurred, but proceeded in a manner which, while being flexible and eclectic, was nevertheless orderly and systematic.

The sheer volume and diversity of the data collected by the team made it necessary to organize it into smaller homogeneous units of information in order to begin to make sense of it. Consequently, the project, by means of the reflective process described above, arranged the data into 'segments' of material based on an organizing system derived from the data themselves. The process, therefore, was essentially one of inductive cross-case analysis (Miles and Huberman 1994), the main outcome of which was a two-dimensional matrix with issues and themes related to school leadership on one axis and the different sources of evidence (i.e. headteachers, governors, parents etc.) on the other. In the early stages of this process the organizing categories, especially the issues and themes, were regarded as being tentative and provisional and were subsequently modified in the search for a more satisfactory system – though it would be difficult to disagree with Lofland (1971) who concluded that 'no order fits perfectly'. Manipulating the fieldwork data in this way proved to be a time-consuming and intellectually exacting activity.

Having arranged the data for purposes of analysis in such a way, it was possible to compare what the different sources of evidence (i.e. headteachers, deputies, governors etc.) had revealed about leadership in their schools, or what a particular category of stakeholder had to say about different aspects of leadership. In the event it was decided that the richness of the insights provided by the analysis of the different perspectives of the various stakeholders interviewed should be reflected in the way in which the research was reported. Consequently, Chapters 3–6 offer one way of viewing the qualitative evidence on leadership in schools, i.e. through the 'angle of observation' provided by headteachers, deputy heads, teachers, support staff, governors, parents and students whose 'voices' and insights the project had tried hard to capture.

However, while the process of inductive analysis which enabled these pictures to be drawn consisted of deconstructing the data, the ultimate objective of the research was a synthesis of the project's empirical evidence with the theoretical constructs on leadership in schools which are already available in the literature. In other words, the aim was to go beyond what Hycner (1985) called a 'composite summary' and what Patton (1980) has referred to as a descriptive account of 'patterns and themes'. Instead the final goal was to offer a critique of existing theories of effective leadership in schools in the light of the project's empirical findings and to suggest some 'provisional' hypotheses (Turner 1981), new concepts or 'theoretical categories' (Lazarsfeld 1972) and some tentative thoughts on 'substantive theory' (Glaser and Strauss 1967).

The analysis eventually developed along two distinct strands. First, the process of thematic induction began to build into a picture of the characteristics and behaviours associated with effective leadership as viewed from the perspectives of the key stakeholders. At the same time, the research team was searching for ways of encapsulating the perspective provided by the headteachers themselves. Although it would have been possible to have drawn upon the characteristics and behaviours described by the headteachers, these did not seem to capture adequately their day-to-day experience of leadership. It was at this point that the team began to develop the idea of using the tensions and dilemmas which headteachers themselves had raised during the interviews. On further examination, the idea of dilemmas proved to be especially attractive because it seemed to encapsulate much of the problematic nature of leadership. It also provided a link between the construction of leadership by the various stakeholders and the individual theories of headteachers – a link based on the overlapping needs and expectations of those surrounding the headteachers and their own beliefs and values. Dilemmas, therefore, offered the prospect of gaining new insights into the difficulties which headteachers have in navigating their way through a complex matrix of expectations while maintaining their personal integrity.

In addition, the adoption of this approach allowed the team to bring together aspects of several of the case studies in a holistic format. No one headteacher encountered all the chosen dilemmas and only a few all aspects of even one of them. What the field evidence showed was that they had all experienced aspects of each dilemma. The analysis allowed these fragments to be drawn together around shared incidents, values and expectations, and in so doing it began to reveal how the headteachers were being positioned by those around them and were positioning themselves.

By presenting the analysis in the form of dilemmas, it was hoped that they would aid further reflection, not just on the nature of leadership, but on the experience of leadership. It is impossible adequately to capture that experience in its totality and the dilemmas do not attempt to do so. Rather they provide a structure for considering how the experience of being a leader arises from the complex interaction of personal ideologies, relationships with staff and students, and the demands of the school situation.

However, given the insights provided by the interviews with headteachers into the impact of their professional work on their personal lives, it would have been worthwhile, on reflection, to have pursued this matter further by questioning those people who are closest to them personally – their partners and friends who know them well. The original research design did not anticipate that this particular perspective might be a valid and potentially fruitful source of evidence.

3

THE HEADTEACHERS

Although the heads were at different stages in their careers, of different ages and different experiences, there were a number of common themes which emerged in answer to questions about their roles, their understandings of leadership and management, their job satisfaction, the changing contexts and challenges of their work, their achievements, their own development and the values which underpinned their work. Each one provided a fascinating biographical account (Ribbins and Sherratt 1992). Collectively they reveal a complex picture of leadership which, although it relates to certain of the theories contained within existing literature, cannot easily be contained within them. All recognized that both leadership and management qualities and skills were necessary to exercise effective leadership, that the possession of management skills would in itself be insufficient to ensure effective leadership and that good leaders need to be both visionary and strategic. It was 'up to the head to take an holistic view. Management is about putting the structures and procedures in place to realise the vision' (Primary head).

Leadership and management must coincide; leadership makes sure that the ship gets to the right place; management makes sure that the ship (crew and cargo) is well run. If it's just your vision you will not get to the right place – you must have a combined agreed vision with all the staff on board. You must have a strategy, therefore, for getting agreement.

(Infant head)

Leadership is about getting across to the staff where we are now and where we are going. It is not about the mechanisms by which that vision is achieved – that is management. Leadership is also about knowing what to do and being able to raise the morale of the staff.

(Secondary head)

The responses of the heads are presented through five broad themes:

• the person in the professional;
• the leader;
• the manager;
• costs and benefits;
• metaphors of self.

The person in the professional: linking personal ideology and educational practice

Leadership is the personal qualities that you bring to the relationships that you are dealing with and the way you expect things to be done.

(Secondary head)

Values

The vision and practices of these heads were organized around a number of core personal values concerning the modelling and promotion of respect (for individuals), fairness and equality, caring for the well-being and whole development of students and staff, integrity and honesty. These core values were part of strong humanitarian or religious ethics which linked their personal and professional selves. These linkages provide empirical support for those who write of the centrality of moral purposes to those involved in teaching:

I have a core belief in equal opportunities for all and I try to let this determine my leadership style. I believe in fairness and equality for pupils. I try and demonstrate this by treating staff and pupils with courtesy and kindness but ultimately I try and demonstrate that the school is a place where everyone has the same chance to succeed.

(Secondary head)

I live by my Christian beliefs and I try to run this school by Christian values. I love the pupils, the teachers and this community. That is what I live out and that is what this school represents for me, a loving community of people. I care deeply about the children and the staff and I try to show this in everything I do.

(Infant head)

Charm and charisma are qualities which get you so far but hard and fast core values and beliefs carry you further . . .

(Secondary head)

Sockett (1993) defines four dimensions of the professional role of teachers: community (which provides a framework of relationships); knowledge or expertise (with technique subservient to moral criteria); accountability (to individuals and the public); and ideals (only by seeing the interplay between ideals of service, purposes and practices can the professional comprehend the moral role). It was clear from everything said by the heads that their leadership values and visions were primarily moral (i.e. dedicated to the welfare of staff and students, with the latter at the centre) rather than primarily instrumental (for economic reasons) or non-educative (for custodial reasons). Their values and visions both constructed their relationships with staff and students and were constructed within them:

What is delivered must be good enough for my own children; people are important . . . respect their views, opinions, feelings and values . . . make sure that every child gets a fair chance . . . be true to one's self . . .

(Primary head)

[I want] to lead the school philosophically, to set down its overall goals, to detail its directions. These are based on a desire to see all pupils grow into autonomous adults, able to achieve independence and excellence but, at the same time, being fully aware of the needs of others and their responsibility towards them.

(Primary head)

I give the same messages to all – pupils, parents, staff, governors and the community – that this school is about honesty, trust and integrity.

(Secondary head)

Vision

It's like a puzzle. If one bit's missing it's not complete.

(Infant head)

The visions expressed by the heads were of their schools at their best. They took account of current and predicted change in economic, social and educational policies and of changing home circumstances of students but rather than being limited by them, asserted the need for the school community itself to build and communicate its values, its commitment to a particular code of behaviour:

It's commitment to a particular code of behaviour, to know how to do one's job, to be prepared continuously to think how to do the job better, to have a commitment to the people who I have a responsibility to. It's all about accountability which I take very seriously. Doesn't matter to me if it's a cleaner who comes in for two hours or a class teacher because to my mind they all have an equally important role.

(Infant head)

The heads were communicating a moral vision for their schools in terms of the nature of the relationship with it. Vision was an inherent part of their leadership relationships in that it helped them communicate a sense of direction for the school:

Leadership is about being visionary – the direction in which you are going and sharing that with others (but not dictating it to them). Vision is about how your beliefs can be translated into actions.

(Primary head)

Leadership is about communicating your vision, how things need to be done. So it's about personal qualities, communication, vision and keeping on course, keeping the overview, keeping the big picture.

(Secondary head)

I think it's important for a head to have vision, to see the whole game. You have to be ahead of the rest and see the overall picture, otherwise you won't be able to manage effectively.

(Primary head)

Integrity

The headteachers communicated their vision and values through relationships with staff and students but they built these around values such as integrity and steadiness of purpose:

I think it's important to have integrity and to show integrity. As a head you have to live by both.

(Secondary head)

I wanted, as a teacher, to make a difference. As a head, I can make that difference greater. However, in order to do so I must stick to my values and have a steadiness of purpose . . . You have to stick to what's important . . . We have managed to retain a broad and balanced curriculum but with the rapid changes it is becoming more and more difficult to hold true to what you believe in.

(Primary head)

At the end of the day the head has to have integrity and . . . to stick to core values and beliefs. It is important that the head can demonstrate integrity in the face of adversity and can show a moral purpose against all odds.

(Primary head)

Care and support

As their personal values were a vital aspect of themselves as leaders so their leadership relationships were based on integrity, to person and to professional:

I don't like to see the join between the official curriculum, classroom schooling and care . . . All the edges are blurred as far as I'm concerned.

(Primary head)

The well-being of the staff and the children is the most important thing.

(Infant head)

It's important that we are able to support one another personally as well as professionally . . . If they have an emergency or crisis at home, I'm going to respond to that . . . so that they feel valued as a person as well as a teacher.

(Primary head)

Belief in the staff that I've got around me is an immense help . . . They're my people that I pastorally look after . . . There is that sort of rapport . . . very rarely do I have to throw my weight around . . . I have never known less tension in a working group of professional people.

(Primary head)

They valued these relationships and in particular the importance which they attached to building self-esteem and restoring self-confidence as the key to successful improvement efforts. They recognized also the important part played by praise:

One thing we did in raising the esteem of the school was raising the esteem of teachers.

(Primary head)

I spend a lot of time saying, 'Thank you very much for doing that. That was a really good job.'

(Infant head)

I try to make sure that I tell them when they've done something good, and try to acknowledge it with parents and governors.

(Primary head)

Commitment

Modelling the kinds of relationships they wanted to develop involved not only expressions of their values and visions but also their commitment. All the heads expressed their enthusiasm and zest for life, regardless of age and experience; every day was a challenge for them, and every achievement added to this commitment:

> I feel if I give 100 per cent my staff will give me 100 per cent. So I work hard and play hard.
>
> > (Primary head)

> I love coming to work. I love the atmosphere, the school. It's something we've all built together, through ourselves, the governors, the parents . . . There's still a lot of fire in my belly for the job.
>
> > (Primary head)

> Every day I am blessed to spend another day with these children . . . It is rewarding and life-affirming.
>
> > (Infant head)

They remained excited by the challenges and opportunities created by change:

> I enjoy the job and the challenge even though the rate of change is so rapid. I like the idea of being the leader of learning. Children now have a range of opportunities in the world and I have a chance to provide them with more . . . I want them to be excited by the possibilities open to them when they leave.
>
> > (Primary head)

> Every day's a challenge . . . I've no wishes to do anything other than what I'm doing . . . Over the years, enthusiasm seems to grow rather than wane. There's an awful lot that I don't think I've done. Where we are now is in a position where we are striving to be better than yesterday.
>
> > (Primary head)

The leader

Relationship-centred

It is difficult to run a school unless you know your staff, so my first job when I arrived was to interview each member of staff. I collected a lot of personal insight and still try to build up personal knowledge of the staff where I can and where it is not intrusive. After all, we are all people and like to know someone cares.

(Infant head)

The most important aspect of leadership for all the heads concerned working successfully with people, establishing the kinds of relationships in which their leadership could be expressed. Being a head was not a 'desk job', though it involved organizational and administrative skills. It was about displaying relationship-centred qualities and skills. Recent research in England on business leaders has revealed the importance to their staff of vision, trust, credibility, support for staff, and collaboration (Tampoe 1998).

It's enabling other people . . . to take over, to do things . . . It's being able to trust other people. To be confident in your own ability . . . to delegate tasks and know they will be done . . . to allow people to do things and not to try and control it all.

(Special school head)

I see leadership as being the front person of the organization, fighting our corner and coming up with certain broad ideas that are then managed . . . It's to do with supporting staff and people feeling that I will support them. It's to do with motivating and appreciating staff's efforts . . . being interested in what they're doing and giving them feedback on a daily basis . . . For them to feel there is somebody who they trust to go out there and give a good account of themselves . . . the feeling that I'm not going to do them down . . . to patrol the boundaries.

(Infant head)

You don't achieve things on your own. You set the way forward, lead by example, communicate what needs to be done and have to be hands on in the way you want it achieved . . . we should always guard against getting a bit complacent.

(Primary head)

Professional standards

By definition good leaders are not only enthusiastic about their
jobs and the potential and achievements of the organization in
which they work; they are also believers in their own judgement:

> I wouldn't ask them to do anything I wouldn't tackle. I think
> sometimes I ask too much or expect too much. That can be
> difficult because I have quite high standards and I'm not
> necessarily patient.

> (Infant head)

Within the group of heads this belief was married to their
ruthlessness in establishing high expectations, an awareness of
the need to think strategically and, on occasions, a willingness
to take risks to do so – though these were based upon an
intimate knowledge of their own constituency. They shared a
self-belief which enabled them to have confidence in their own
judgements:

> Knowing what I think is good for the school and being able
> to discard what I think is not.

> (Secondary head)

> A head has to have the ability to analyse problems and
> work out solutions quickly (but not on one's own). To do this
> he has to be intellectually capable of thinking and making
> judgements on his feet.

> (Secondary head)

This self-belief was often complemented and interleaved with a
strong sense of standards and achievement:

> Underachievement is not acceptable. The nettle must be
> grasped.

> (Secondary head)

The sense of direction combined with relationship-centred
leadership which all the heads practised was related to their
determination that all students and teachers should strive for
high standards of behaviour and attainment. They achieved this
through a combination of high expectations and teamwork. This
meant a continuing pressure on self and others for improvement
– and this, it seemed, was not based on standards imposed
externally:

The schooling provided [here] has to be good enough for my own children, and if this is the case then it should be fine for other parents. This means that when a child is here there should be no closed doors in their world. They should be excited by the opportunities presented to them, especially having a broad, balanced and well-taught curriculum. Directives from the government are likely to restrict what a school can offer, but you must not let this dominate.

(Primary head)

My aims with regard to this school are . . . to get the best out of every child, not just academically through improved examination results but through their achievements in music, sport etc.

(Secondary head)

I want all the pupils to achieve fluency in literacy and numeracy. Even small steps taken by the less able give me great satisfaction.

(Primary head)

The school stands for high expectations, good quality of life for all the people in the school, so that the people who work here are contented in what they are doing, feel valued, can meet the expectations.

(Primary head)

Defined by the achievement of their staff

Pupils must be expected to achieve to the maximum of their potential and I look to the staff to produce the best teaching to enable them to do that.

(Secondary head)

The shared high expectations and determination of the heads to achieve the highest possible standards almost always meant that they were pushing themselves and their staff to the limits. Previous practices were rarely good enough. Indeed, many heads had often inherited situations in which achievement levels of staff and students were unacceptably low. They spoke of these and the progress made:

When the previous head left . . . the situation was one of conflict, lack of direction . . . the staff were defensive, wary

and suspicious of the new head. Eight years later we have a
professional and cohesive staff with a sense of direction – it
was a matter of liberating their potential. It was good to
have what has been achieved validated by Ofsted.

(Primary head)

Students' backgrounds were taken into account but not used
as a reason for lowering expectations of achievement:

The staff I have now have high expectations of themselves.
Although I take responsibility with the governors for setting
standards there is not one member of staff who says to me,
'These children can't do this' any more. When I first came
here I had little deputations from each of the teachers in turn,
'Of course you know we're on the Estate and you can't
expect . . .'. I felt, 'Yes, some of the children who come here
do have problems and that undoubtedly does affect their
education, but that is no reason why we should not expect
to do something about it.' I think that is how all the staff
feel now, a very positive, 'You throw it at us and we'll do it
and do it well.'

(Infant head)

All recognized the need to 'push' the limits, both in terms of
themselves and staff and pupils:

The achievement here is that we really push ourselves to
the limits to get there . . . We know we have further to go
in pushing the children and I think we are doing that, and
they are not unhappy . . . There has to be a balance because
children have to have time to have fun.

(Primary head)

We are in a situation where we are striving to do better
than yesterday because we are very confident in what we
do . . . We've got the expertise and teacher power to do it.

(Primary head)

Outwards looking in: being ahead of the game

Insularity was something the headteachers fought against. In
the busy worlds of classrooms and schools, as they sought to
manage imposed change and create the kinds of cultures that

matched their visions, they maintained their awareness of what was happening beyond their own environments, partly to gather intelligence related to the latest developments in policy and practice. This enabled them to be proactive rather than reactive to external change:

> I'm somebody who will look at other schools . . . and listen to colleagues from across the country . . . There is a cross-fertilization all the time of ideas. I think that benefits the school immensely because you hear, you see, you listen, you analyse what other people are doing to make their school successful, or, on the other hand, unsuccessful . . . Outwards looking in is often better than sitting in and not looking out . . . I think I'm something of a squirrel or magpie.
>
> (Primary head)

> In the past year I have got more involved outside the school . . . It gives me a wider perspective. I'm enjoying getting the bigger picture . . . contact with other heads is essential . . . you pick up what's going on, how they are dealing with issues. I take time to go out and make those sorts of contacts now, whereas in the early days I was probably very busy, inward, getting things off the ground.
>
> (Primary head)

> I think part of the role of a head is the same as that of a managing director – to network, network and network.
>
> (Primary head)

> I keep my ears to the ground via my support networks for the sake of the staff . . . I see the role of the head as listening to a multiplicity of problems and points of view and communicating with people both on and off the premises.
>
> (Primary head)

> I frequently refer to relevant books . . . to ensure that I am in a position to inform correctly all concerned before going forward. Every step has to be checked before going ahead and I use well-referenced arguments to deal with people [in the context of dealing with LEA, media, unions, parent, representatives].
>
> (Special school head)

You're looking at government papers, you're reading, talking,
listening to other people ... or you might be sitting in the
bar [at a conference] at night ... but you're looking back
into your own school and thinking, 'Will that work?' or, 'Isn't
that a good idea?' or, 'Thank God I don't do it that way'.

(Primary head)

As part of the process of 'managing uncertainty', these heads
were also willing to take risks for the good of the school:

I'm prepared to take chances ... that I think will improve
my school ... I don't overly concern myself with bits of
paper.

(Primary head)

I think all heads are essentially risk takers if they are good
heads ... We need to take risks to ensure that we obtain
the best for pupils and staff.

(Primary head)

I am always prepared to give things a try even if they are
not always successful – it is the trying which is important.

(Primary head)

In the community

Forming and maintaining positive working relationships within
their local communities was a priority for all the heads:

... there's a strong link between the school and the church
... I have also cultivated links with other faiths e.g. a Hindu
is a governor and a Muslim parent provides me with a link
to the mosque.

(Infant head)

I do all I can in liaison with parents, governors, social and
welfare agencies, LEA [Local Education Authority], HMI [Her
Majesty's Inspectors], civic and commercial leaders to take
the school forward with confidence so that it is met with
equal trust and confidence.

(Primary head)

We work as closely with parents as we can.

(Primary head)

We have worked hard to promote ourselves.

(Primary head)

We work very closely with the local FE [Further Education] College . . . We have lecturers in the school on a pilot 'Learning Assistance' programme. They come in and work with teachers in the classroom and run courses for parents.

(Primary head)

Such community links often stretched to exchanges with schools and businesses in Europe, America and New Zealand and communication to parents through newsletters. Aided schools especially expressed a particularly strong bond with their communities. These strategic drives which were a central part of all the heads' working lives were matched by an equal determination to achieve high standards and a low tolerance level for those who did not 'sign on' to this agenda.

'Tough love'

If unpleasant things have to be done [with regard to improving classroom teaching] I don't shrink from it because I realize that I am likely to be improving matters and doing it for the good of the children.

(Primary head)

Leading and managing change is complex and time-consuming, and, because change means more work and additional responsibilities, it requires leaders to be tough-minded:

I try to be a good mediator by being sympathetic to all points of view. However, I am not frightened to go one way or the other and make a decision even though it might not be popular.

(Primary head)

A teacher's weakness is no resource. There's no point in waffling around the edges. It wasn't a knee-jerk reaction on my part. Nothing was happening [in a particular department] . . . it was affecting the esteem of the school. We did a thorough inspection using Ofsted criteria. It was pretty sad. One teacher resigned. She was so bitter. This caused tremendous wobbles in the staffroom.

(Secondary head)

I think of myself as a caring head but if someone attacks me
or threatens to hurt my school and the people in it, I can be
very tough indeed.

(Secondary head)

We are a small school, we are a very friendly staff, we work
very hard, we laugh an awful lot. So we have a good cama-
raderie. But at the same time, that laughter doesn't mean
that [deputy] and I don't have to put on the professional
guise and sometimes the things we have to say aren't necessarily that popular.

(Infant head)

If we come to an impasse I will say, 'You've got to do it . . .'
and, 'You've had your debate and I've seen the pros and
cons and this is the way it's going to be done.' Then I'll
walk away and they'll accept.

(Secondary head)

Though aware that some of their actions might not be popular
with all staff or parents at all times, they were unafraid of tem-
porary unpopularity:

You look for people who are interested, who have got your
ideas. You get people on board who will stick with you and
then you look for those people who are on the borderline,
on the fence. You also identify people that are going to be
downright awkward and not want the ideas in place
because they are in their own . . . comfort zones . . . You make
enemies . . . but you've not got to be bothered whether you're
liked or disliked . . . You like to be liked but . . .

(Secondary head)

Pupils, staff and parents have to see a person of quality and
warmth who will not be afraid to 'rollick' people if he has
to. They need a real person.

(Primary head)

Their determination to be tough for the good of the pupils
was, however, accompanied by a focus upon taking colleagues
with them:

You have to be clear in your own mind where you want to
go in the end [but] you have to be flexible and take on

board and be seen to be using [the staff's] suggestions . . . so that people can feel that we've arrived at this together . . . it's essential that you take your colleagues with you.

(Secondary head)

A good team who work well together . . . given the opportunities for things they wanted to pursue . . . develop things, where they needed to develop professionally . . .

(Primary head)

The manager

Organizational health is seen as key to the effectiveness and improvement of schools. We have seen already how good heads commit themselves to the 'juggling act' of leadership which means innumerable meetings, active involvement in local, regional, national and sometimes international communities and considerable personal social and emotional investment in individual staff and students' lives. Schools, though, also have to be managed. There were three features of management common to all these heads:

- a proactive concern with recruitment and selection of staff;
- an abiding focus upon monitoring teaching, learning and achievement; and
- an active interest in the continuing professional development of staff.

Recruitment and selection of staff

All the heads were proactive in this, regarding it as a key to developing their vision and creating and maintaining conditions for the kinds of culture necessary to enable staff and students to be fully motivated and achieve their potential:

Finding the best-suited person for teaching jobs is very important . . . I am prepared to travel to see candidates teaching in their present schools to assess their suitability for a particular job . . . It is worth the cost and you are less likely to make a recruitment error which could be more costly in the long term.

(Primary head)

The selection of all staff must be an abiding concern. They should be supported in their career aspirations and they must be supported in their everyday work.

(Primary head)

We do try and select staff who know what we are about and how we are going to work . . . They are appointed to be people who will have ideas and want to make changes, because hopefully most of the people I have appointed will want to move on, people who will be fairly ambitious and therefore put a lot into the school.

(Infant head)

Monitoring – 'one of the most difficult jobs I do'

One of the most difficult jobs I do is to monitor the school's performance. It is a tricky business really judging how we are doing on a regular basis.

(Primary head)

Monitoring was perceived as one of their most difficult jobs, for the heads recognized that it was not entirely a rational process. Because it was tied to targets, standards and achievement it inevitably impinged on the heart of every teacher's professional identity and self-esteem. It needed, therefore, to be underpinned by a close personal knowledge of staff, pupils and parents.

I am constantly assessing their [the staff's] strengths and weaknesses – how they relate to children, which is the best range for them to teach . . . You can only make the right decisions if you know your staff personally. I talk a lot to the pupils individually and by doing this and four out of the five dinner duties, I get to know them at a social level. I know the names of the vast majority of pupils . . . and I pride myself in this.

(Primary head)

I walk around the school . . . I am around all the time so that I can support staff or anyone immediately.

(Secondary head)

There are well-planned observations, monitoring and evaluation by colleagues . . . Every fortnight the three teachers in

each year [with 'phase' responsibilities for curriculum] sit
down together to evaluate and plan.

(Secondary head)

Monitoring itself was for three purposes – to identify the need
for remediation, to check that standards were being maintained
and objectives met, and to assess the continuing professional
development (CPD) needs of staff.

Continuing professional development

Allowing teachers to be professional is going to become
increasingly harder. Maintaining staff morale will be the main
area of need for heads in the future.

(Primary head)

All the heads consistently and vigorously promoted all forms
of staff development whether through in-service training, visits
to other schools, or peer support schemes. Their two principal
concerns were maintaining morale and motivation and capacity
building:

It is now more important than ever to educate the staff –
they need both new knowledge and CPD. We are working
with the Industrial Society on the idea of 'liberation management' which involves the empowerment of staff at all levels
and building effective teams.

(Secondary head)

It was noticeable, also, that such development did not only
focus upon needs which were of direct benefit to the school and
classroom but also those which were of direct benefit to the
individual as a person, and that the development needs of non-
teaching staff were also included. In a sense, the emphasis which
the heads placed on the continuing development of their staff
reflected a recognition that the teachers were their most important
asset and that, particularly in times of change, it was important
to maintain their own sense of self-worth by valuing them:

I tell the staff to bring their problems to me with their preferred solutions and their analysis of its ramifications – in
this way the staff are educated throughout their day-to-day
work.

(Primary head)

I aim to achieve cohesiveness among the staff. I hope that the staff have a sense of direction and opportunities to do what they want to do and feel secure and confident in that. I always try to respect the individual . . . hopefully, if I am respectful of their views and opinions, it will make them feel valued.

(Secondary head)

Heads themselves acted as role models:

I enrolled in the doctorate because I cannot persuade staff to invest in their own professional development unless I invest in mine.

(Secondary head)

All were active in intervening to promote capacity and growth:

So I said, 'Neither of you are going to do extraneous duties, which clears seventeen hours each week. It gives you a bit of space.'

(Special school head)

Teachers need not only support but clear guidance. Most of the things we work through . . . we start with interest groups and we work upwards towards the whole school.

(Secondary head)

If people just sit there that's fine. They can't grow unless somebody acts, and I think that is one of the things that has helped me progress, having someone to question me.

(Special school head)

Many, also, recognized the need in themselves for a 'critical friend':

You want someone to say, 'Wait a minute, have you really thought this through?' To question me is better for the school. It stops my weaknesses having such an effect on the school as they might have done . . . The need to be challenged, to have your ideas put under pressure.

(Primary head)

There were many stories of heads supporting staff in pursuing what might be regarded by some as 'non-school-related' agendas.

For example, time out of school was given in order to ease a teacher's participation in a sporting event. Another teacher was provided with support for the resolution of a personal problem. In these and other stories the direct benefit to the individuals was, according to the heads, more than repaid at later dates in their added commitment to out-of-school activities – though there was no explicit 'quid pro quo' agreement that this should be the case. In all instances, too, it was a personal knowledge of the head and a mutual respect which enabled these unusual CPD opportunities to occur.

Phase of development

Finally in this section it is worth noting that, like teachers, heads will be in different development phases which will affect the way they work (Day and Bakioğlu 1996; Reeves *et al.* 1997). Their expertise grows and may decline over time. Note how these heads reflected on the changes in their approaches to leadership:

> I've grown slower and calmer. I've become less manic about wanting change.
>
> (Primary head)

> I am less anxious about change than I was when I first arrived. I have become better at managing change and encouraging others to engage in that process.
>
> (Special school head)

> In the early days [1989] it was more cut and dried. We're going to do this and this. You've got to dictate in the early days . . . Now I listen much more to people . . . you can take an elder statesman role when somebody comes up with an idea and . . . you can remember doing it 25 years ago . . . Once you've established yourself you can be a little more of a democratic leader and . . . give people their head . . . When you are struggling in the early days of getting an organization sorted out you can't afford too many mistakes.
>
> (Primary head)

> When you first come into post there is this horrible feeling that you have to hold everything together and . . . gradually you get to know people and you have the confidence to

value other people's opinions, to relax. You also get an idea
of how you want to work.

(Secondary head)

The best time was at the end of five years. A lot had been
achieved . . . development of initiatives like curriculum co-
ordination, appraisal and staff development. Seven years on
I'm a lot stronger than I was and say, 'I've learnt how to do
it and now you'll just have to put up with me.'

(Primary head)

Over the years, enthusiasm seems to grow rather than wane.
The pace of life within the school has increased 100 per
cent, but you learn to live with the pace . . . I think I have
more faith in the staff . . . There's an awful lot that I don't
think I've done.

(Primary head)

Costs and benefits

Enormous amounts of time and energy were invested in building the kinds of collaborative cultures inside and outside the
school which were consistent with the heads' values and visions
and which contributed to their fulfilment. This created inevitable tensions caused either by recalcitrant or uncommitted staff,
by new policy changes, or simply by the challenge of maintaining energy under stressful conditions in the constant quest for
improvement.

*The management of stress – 'being accountable to
everyone and being blamed for everything'*

All the heads worked long hours and played a variety of complex
proactive and reactive roles:

The job has no boundaries so you must impose your own to
maintain your sanity.

(Primary head)

The simultaneity and complexity of the job . . . make for a
long agenda for the day – and often, however hard you
have worked, it has not altered very much by the end.

(Secondary head)

They talked of the ways in which they managed to survive:

I don't take things deadly seriously. I see things come across my desk, I look at them and put them in the bin . . . No one comes back to you about any of this.

(Primary head)

I have a totally efficient school secretary who deals with all the stuff I don't have to bother with.

(Infant head)

I don't take masses of work home with me. I skim through the mail in the morning (arrives 6–7 a.m.) and the rest of the time is mine.

(Primary head)

Support networks of family and friends and keeping physically fit were also vital in 'taking them out' of their focus on school:

I couldn't do this job if I wasn't fit and healthy.

(Infant head)

I don't seem to have to take problems home much. I'm able to wind down . . . I've got a very supportive family.

(Primary head)

I'm part of a headteacher support group. We take turns in discussing issues . . . A difficult thing I had to learn which maybe isn't common to everybody is that you don't have to do the job 24 hours a day. You're entitled to stop and have a reasonable amount of time for yourself and in fact it's better for the school.

(Secondary head)

I have to tell myself that I can't be all things to all people all the time and not to cross bridges before I have to.

(Secondary head)

All spoke of the demands of excessive bureaucracy upon their time and energy:

I have to work hard all the time – from early morning on school days – and to do the job properly I still have to complete the paperwork at the weekends . . . I have returned to school in the evening 40 times this school year for work purposes.

(Primary head)

There is too much paperwork to cope with and because it cannot just be 'filed away' it means that I cannot attend to the children as much as I would like. I have a sense of failing constantly . . . Because tasks take much longer there is not enough time to do everything. Therefore, lower order tasks go to the bottom of priorities – or, even worse, are neglected altogether.

(Primary head)

Because of the amount of paperwork I have a feeling of failure because I can't meet my own agenda and feel constrained by events . . . But I have great support from my family – they often 'manage' me to relieve my stress by making the meal in the evening, taking me out to the cinema . . . I also use stress management strategies taken from an LEA course – not taking work home some evenings for a change, deciding what has to be done in terms of what is most important and doing things only as and when it is required for the welfare of the school.

(Secondary head)

Metaphors

Heads characterized themselves as

multifaceted diamonds . . . tough inside, which means steadiness of purpose and sticking to one's values in the face of pressures not to do so . . .

(Primary head)

or captains of the ship,

steering through or away from adversaries, confronting the unavoidable in the front line, not from a distance . . . an armchair spider controlling the web . . .

(Primary head)

or

film directors; you've got your deputy who's like a producer. You've both got different roles and you're trying to help the actors give their best performance . . . but at the end of the day it's all about the audience – here it's the children . . .

(Infant head)

Another described herself as

> bossy . . . pretty strong personality . . . like action . . . always like to be in the driving seat . . . thinking I could do it . . . always like small schools . . . saw myself as a 'Sybil Marshall' . . .
>
> (Infant head)

Others were more

> democratic . . . being open and communicative, consultative with people and empowering staff at all levels – but not to the extent that decisions are not made quickly and decisively . . .
>
> (Secondary head)

or being

> team players . . . but leading from the front. The image I have is of being part of the team but being team captain. I don't see myself as set apart from the school but part of it . . .
>
> (Special school head)

One head described herself as

> a servant leader . . . serving the school on behalf of God and not myself. He guides me in my work and assists me in my leadership role.
>
> (Infant head)

Conclusion

The interviews provided by the heads highlighted the busyness, intensity and complexity of their fragmented working lives. They worked long hours, were 'on call' and spent large parts of their time in face-to-face meetings with a range of stakeholders. They were almost always 'on show' and in the public eye. This visibility inevitably caused tensions and, occasionally, ill health. However, what characterized all the heads was their resilience, their sheer capacity for hard work and their continuing adherence, under all circumstances, to their vision for the kind of school which would provide the best opportunities for the learning and achievement of all pupils and staff.

Given the richness of the information provided about themselves as leaders, managers and people, it is difficult to subscribe to mechanistic, rationalistic-oriented models of headship or to those texts which suggest that one 'style' or leadership approach provides better results than another. It was clear, for example, that these heads were neither 'transformational' or 'transactional' in the normal sense of their use; though it was equally clear that all had changed their schools for the better. They continued to make a difference to the lives of students, staff and community and did so principally through the strength, integrity and perseverance of their core beliefs and vision of education, their high levels of intra- and interpersonal qualities and skills, their ability to manage competing demands, tensions and dilemmas, and their capacities to continue to be enthusiastic about the learning and achievement of staff and students in changing times.

4

THE DEPUTIES AND TEACHERS

THE DEPUTIES

In all the schools within the study, deputies were asked to comment upon the leadership and management approaches adopted by their respective headteachers. Given the increasing research evidence concerning the pivotal role of the senior management team in maintaining an effective school, the deputy heads' views on headship were particularly pertinent. Their perspectives on leadership style also offered an important point of cross-reference with the headteachers' data. This provided a secure basis upon which to consider subsequent data sets.

Despite a wide variation of practice among the individual heads, there was a high degree of consensus about the general features of effective leadership. A number of key themes emerged from the data that illustrated and defined effective leadership in practice. These themes are presented under a set of headings that broadly reflect those in the previous chapter.

Leadership and management

There is a clear distinction in the literature between leadership and management (e.g. West-Burnham 1997). Leadership relates to vision, direction and inspiration while management is about planning, getting things done and working effectively with people. When deputies were asked to comment upon this distinction, they identified vision as a core component of effective leadership. While they were able to distinguish between leadership and management functions, there was a consistent view that leadership was centrally about realizing the head's vision of the school:

> Leadership is about having a vision of how the school should improve to progress; management is about the means by which that vision is achieved; people other than the head share in the shaping of the vision.
>
> (Primary deputy)

> Leadership and management overlap, but prime responsibility for leadership rests with the head – when she is absent an experienced deputy can do the management. Leadership involves inspiring others, as well as developing and supporting them – that requires skill and confidence.
>
> (Secondary deputy)

> Leadership is about having vision and articulating, ordering priorities, getting others to go with you, constantly reviewing what you are doing and holding on to things you value. Management is about the functions, procedures and systems by which you realize the vision.
>
> (Primary deputy)

> He is quite complex because he has the ability to go out in front and barge around and do things . . . but there's an underlying insecurity which goes along with very clear vision and inspirational leadership . . . His strong beliefs and values influence what he does.
>
> (Primary deputy)

Visions are about hopes and possibilities; in short, a better future. The study found that heads provided a sense of direction and concern for the future. One deputy summed this up by saying:

That's the thing I like about him. He is always looking to the future, how we can improve, what can we do here, what new ideas can you get from this.

(Primary deputy)

Fullan (1992a: 37) suggests that vision building 'permeates the organisation with values, purpose and integrity for both the what and how of improvement' but adds, 'it is never an easy concept to work with largely because its formulation, implementation, shaping and re-shaping in specific organisations is a constant process'. The deputies reinforced the fact that vision building is a highly sophisticated dynamic process:

It's OK to have vision but how do you sustain it over time? How do you take people with you? The head seems to have what it takes and can motivate and mobilize others to believe in her vision.

(Secondary deputy)

There was a general consensus that the heads in the study were good at managing change. As a result of their ability to respond to change through a speedy process of planning and implementation, they were successful in managing change. The deputies recognized that part of the way in which heads managed change was via a process of delegation:

He has to delegate to achieve change – he cannot do it all himself as headteachers were able to do in the past. Over a period of four/five years he has restructured the management of the school in order to deliver the curriculum more effectively. He has tended in the past to respond too quickly to new initiatives (as soon as he has heard the announcements on Radio 4) – he has had to learn to act when the proposed changes have become more definite.

(Primary deputy)

Changes are externally imposed so that the head must interpret incoming documents before she can inform the staff. The speed with which those changes have had to be introduced means that she has had little time to motivate staff and she is finding it increasingly difficult to justify imposing yet more demands for change. It also makes it difficult to

see things through – she has had to learn to delegate more
of the responsibility for managing change.

(Secondary deputy)

With increasing expectations upon schools to respond to externally imposed change, an ever-growing speed of response is required. Clearly, some responsibility for managing and handling
change can be delegated to others within the organization. The
current trend towards participative management would endorse
delegated authority. However, this does not necessarily reduce
the manager's ultimate responsibility. The deputies noted the
important role of the head in keeping an overview of the day-
to-day running of the school. Such routine monitoring was identified as one of the essential management skills for school leaders:

The head has to keep an overall view of what is happening
in the school. He is always monitoring progress and keeping a
check on things. He has to keep his 'finger on the pulse' but
cannot physically do everything – delegation is essential.

(Secondary deputy)

The deputies also recognized that the role of the head in the
last few years had extended beyond that of manager to that of
entrepreneur. They acknowledged that the job demanded more
risk taking than was previously expected and that heads were
expected to introduce innovation and challenge within the
organization:

The role of the head is now one of trouble shooter with an
expectation to lead with entrepreneurial flair and wise business acumen.

(Infant deputy)

Staff expect more of a head these days. He is not just managing the budget but getting involved in fund raising.

(Primary deputy)

It was clear from the data that deputies shared a view that the
role of the head had dramatically changed in the last ten years.
They were of the view that the role was now more demanding and
challenging, placing greater stress upon individuals and greater
demand upon personal resources. However, for those heads who
held strong sets of personal values, there was evidence that this
assisted them in managing some of the tensions of the job.

The person in the professional

One consistent theme that emerged from the data concerned the importance of the core personal values that directly influenced the leadership style of the head. Deputies generally shared a view that the core values held by the head contributed directly to being successful. Deputies talked, for example, about the headteacher holding 'human values' and viewing the school as an 'environment in which staff and pupils should be happy'. These values manifested themselves in a variety of ways but most often deputies described them as being about 'holding high expectations for pupils' and 'encouraging all pupils to achieve'.

High expectations

There is a substantial literature confirming the importance of high expectations as a major factor in school effectiveness (e.g. Sammons *et al.* 1997). In the view of the deputies in the study, the heads held high expectations of pupils and staff. They shared a fundamental commitment to equality of opportunity and a belief that all pupils should and could achieve:

> He wants the pupils to leave primary school at the age of 11 feeling that 'the world is their oyster' – that they can develop in whatever way they wish.
>
> (Primary deputy)

> She believes in: accountability for the pupils' achieving their full potential; that schools should provide a caring and supportive environment in which children can be happy at whatever they are doing; having high expectations of the pupils; professional autonomy of teachers coupled with accountability for their actions.
>
> (Primary deputy)

For some heads these high expectations were evident in the way the school was run and managed:

> He wants it to be a well run school and everybody working as a team . . . He wants everybody to work together for the benefit of the school and the children. He seems to expect the best, no matter what. I think he wants a school that's

not necessarily top of the tables but more importantly he wants a happy school that is well run where people know and are given the information as to what's going on. The children know where they stand with [head's] expectation of discipline. There is a standard expected of everybody whether they are 4 or 11 years old . . .

(Primary deputy)

He knows exactly how he wants his school run . . . how he wants his staff to work. He doesn't expect too much. He's always been incredibly fair . . . he's not one that you feel is watching you every minute and clocking it down. He's very fair and I think the staff recognize and appreciate that . . . He knows the way he expects the children and staff to behave, and he'll let you know . . . He's quite astute.

(Secondary deputy)

For other heads it was their relationship with others that embodied their high expectations:

Very high expectations of everybody . . . believes in children being able to work independently . . . Children as learners, teachers as learners, parents as community . . . being a learning school.

(Infant deputy)

High levels of expectation were also accompanied by the heads' mutual trust and respect of others.

Mutual trust and respect

Deputies commented upon the integrity of their headteachers and the importance of mutual trust and respect in motivating others. This was considered to be particularly important within the relationship between deputy and head. The deputies commented upon the importance of a close working relationship with the head and the centrality of mutual support and confidentiality within this relationship:

As head and deputy we argue and debate so you have to have confidentiality and mutual trust in the head/deputy relationship.

(Primary deputy)

In addition, the deputies commented upon the interpersonal skills of the heads and the fact that they worked hard to understand and care for their staff. Even when personal conflicts arose, it was clear that the heads made every effort to deal with them promptly and fairly:

> She's very good with staff. If there is ever a problem she will talk to them and listen to them and try to help to solve the problem. She understands family problems and personal problems . . . She works her staff extremely hard. At the end of the day she does listen and take [my] views on board and if she didn't I'd think a lot less of her.
>
> (Secondary deputy)

> He's straight as a die with everybody. If there's an upset he'll sort it out and he might be very bombastic and maybe a bit too harsh . . . or handle things off the top of his head a bit too quickly but at the end of the day he's quite caring. He'll always come back and try to smooth over things . . .
>
> (Secondary deputy)

The general view of the heads presented by the deputies was of caring individuals who placed people at the centre of their work.

Person-centredness

The deputies reflected a view of leadership that was 'person-centred' rather then 'task-centred'. Many talked of the personal qualities of the head and their presence and charisma rather than their management competence. It was evident from the data that the headteachers in the study were effective communicators who cared about people and were keen to make any new developments transparent to others:

> That is very much his style, that people understand why things are happening, not just putting them in place. Because they need to know what the expectations are.
>
> (Primary deputy)

In some cases, heads were seen to be good at working with certain groups rather than others. In one or two cases this was seen negatively:

He makes little effort to communicate with people at the
base of the school hierarchy, but he deals with pupil and
parental problems very well, spending much time on them
if necessary.

(Special school deputy)

Generally, however, the deputy heads in the study were com-
plimentary about the interpersonal skills of the headteacher:

She is good in one-to-one situations with parents – responding to their problems, etc.

(Primary deputy)

She is an excellent communicator and listens to others
carefully.

(Infant deputy)

Communication

The ability to communicate was considered to be an important
attribute of the headteacher. Deputies recognized that even though
heads worked hard and held high expectations, communication
with others was still important:

He works *very* hard – though he always finds time to talk to
others.

(Primary deputy)

She works hard – there is a constant flow of information
but everyone is kept informed and feels valued.

(Infant deputy)

A common theme from the deputies concerned the way in which
heads managed the enormous amount of work facing them on a
daily basis. It was evident that heads managed the stress caused
by such pressure in a variety of ways and that often this had a
personal cost.

Costs and benefits

Stress

The consequence of hard work manifested itself as stress in many
of the heads. Deputies commented upon the way in which heads

dealt with stress. This ability to cope with high levels of stress was considered important, although the ways of managing stress differed:

> Goes to the gym regularly each week, but finds it difficult to 'switch off' through social activities. Needs a 'critical friend' on whom he can off-load, especially when new initiatives come in rapid succession – deputy provides but it is a 'two-way street' between them. He attends short courses regularly.
>
> (Primary deputy)

> She has strong support from her family – especially her husband. She also has a network of close friends who support each other and with whom she can release her feelings. The head can be vulnerable and experience a feeling of isolation.
>
> (Primary deputy)

> He has an active social life outside school and has a group of friends with whom he and his wife go hill walking, play bridge and do amateur dramatics. He is an NAHT person and regularly attends their meetings.
>
> (Special school deputy)

> Through his Union work we get a lot of difficult problems ... he finds that challenging ... the work gives him a kind of stability when other things are changing, as they do from time to time, in your personal life ... the work is there to hold onto.
>
> (Primary deputy)

Whichever way heads preferred to manage stress, deputies commented that it was a constant feature of their work. For deputies the challenges that this brought often meant that they also felt pressure and the personal cost of too many demands.

Managing and developing others

Part of the daily pressure experienced by deputies and heads concerned managing others. In dealing with staff, deputies noted that the heads often saw their role as 'liberating others' or giving staff 'professional autonomy'. In some respects, this way of managing staff is consistent with transformational leadership approaches. Deputies commented upon the head as 'head learner' rather than headteacher. CPD was generally given a high priority by the heads, and deputies felt that in most cases staff felt valued and professionally enriched by the leadership of the headteacher:

> The head places a great deal of weight upon the professional development of his staff. His view is that if teachers are boring the pupils are boring!
>
> (Primary deputy)

> He supports the staff and communicates that they are valued and in turn the staff support the head in difficult times. He actively encourages and takes pride in the CPD of his staff.
>
> (Primary deputy)

> All the staff are valued as individuals and he will always listen to them. He has brought them together and they are a cohesive staff. He is aware of the problems of individual children and responds to their needs. He strikes a balance between supporting others and getting on with the things which have to be done.
>
> (Secondary deputy)

The issue of 'support versus challenge' was one that all deputies acknowledged. While they agreed that staff needed to be challenged and that this was best achieved through appropriate staff development programmes, they also recognized the importance of supporting them, particularly in times of crisis.

Supporting staff

A consistent theme within the data concerned the emphasis heads placed upon supporting staff at difficult or traumatic times. A number of deputies commented upon the way in which the headteacher sought to support staff and to ensure they felt valued, even in the most testing circumstances:

> The head aims to provide cohesion for the staff and acknowledges that good communications are important. He recognizes staff achievements and likes the staff to discuss problems with him but expects them to be prepared to offer solutions to those problems.
>
> (Secondary deputy)

At the time of the Ofsted inspection she brought lots of experience to the situation. She was well informed [e.g. through her contacts with other heads] and no one doubted that she would be able to cope with the 'officialdom'. She lived through it with the staff and showed how human she was – she even had a good cry when it was all over!

(Infant deputy)

She takes up professional issues and causes [through the local branch of the NAHT]; she fights for causes; she can be very stubborn (determined?) when she has to be. At times of crisis [e.g. when the media attention was focused on the school] the staff knew that she would cope – the head and the staff were mutually supportive (practically and emotionally).

(Primary deputy)

The deputies commented upon the way in which heads protected and supported staff through difficult times and how this built a sense of community within the school.

Community

The heads in the study shared a deep commitment to developing the community both within and outside the school. Within the school this was generally achieved by developing a sense of collegiality and working collaboratively. Outside, the heads were seen to be active and enthusiastic promoters of the school. The 'networking' skills of the heads were acknowledged to be important as well as their role in public relations:

He uses the local network of headteachers as a source of information and as a means of filtering out what should be brought into the school.

(Primary deputy)

He uses his NAHT contacts to gather and sift information about what to bring back into school.

(Primary deputy)

It was evident that heads in the study were highly skilled at obtaining resources for the school via a variety of means. They utilized local networks for the school's gain and were generally excellent ambassadors on behalf of the school.

Conclusion

Overall, deputies presented a view of the effective headteacher as someone who is highly principled and caring about the role he or she fulfils. In contrast to the transactional leader, the effective heads in the study displayed many characteristics of transformational leadership. For example, kind and caring, willing to empower others, they were good at delegating and trying to transform the school from within. However, as noted already, the notion of the transformational leader does not extend far enough to capture the essence of the headteachers' leadership style in the study. In many respects, the leadership style identified here originates from a core personal set of values and beliefs, premised upon individual integrity and caring.

Set in the context of unprecedented change, it is interesting that headteachers facing such dilemmas operate from a human rather than organizational perspective. In the post-modern world of schooling it would appear that effective headteachers have recognized the limitations of a purely managerialist approach to leadership.

THE TEACHERS

A broad spectrum of teachers were interviewed, from newly qualified primary school teachers to secondary school teachers with careers stretching over twenty years. Collectively they had experienced a wide range of leadership styles and approaches. Many of them had had the opportunity to judge the effectiveness of different types of leaders in a range of schools. When talking about leadership in their schools they drew on these prior experiences. Although their judgements were informed by their previous relationships with headteachers their interest in leadership was not just historical, or academic. The quality of their professional lives, and opportunities for career enhancement, were directly linked to the quality of the leadership in their schools, and their comments related to these aspects. What was more significant, however, was the degree of compassion with which all acknowledged the difficult nature of the headteacher's role.

School structures, policies and the curriculum all offer the possibility for headteachers to demonstrate their leadership. Each have their place in articulating the vision, ethos and values of those who lead, and in establishing their position in an organization. In many of the schools the headteachers had delegated much of the management of these areas to others. Some had done this so that they could find time to teach others because they wanted to develop new initiatives. From the perspective of individual teachers, though, the headteachers expressed their leadership not so much through these 'traditional' avenues as via their direct relationships with staff, their approach to staff development and the way in which they made decisions.

As with the deputies, teachers were asked about leadership and its relationship with management. Teachers could clearly differentiate between the responsibilities and roles of the leader versus the manager.

Leadership and management

For the teachers leadership consisted of providing a role model, giving the school direction, having an overview, setting standards and making 'tough' decisions – all in all what could be described as a relatively traditional view of the role of a leader:

> Leadership is setting the goals and leading by example, but there does come a time when a distance and authority has to be there.
>
> (Primary teacher)

> Whatever you do she sets the example and she has always given more. It doesn't matter how hard you work, you know the same amount will be put in.
>
> (Primary teacher)

> Leadership is about encouraging and motivating the staff, realizing that the head can't do everything and has to delegate, looking to the future, recognizing strengths and building on them and identifying weaknesses and remedying them. It is about being a figurehead, a role model for the staff and the school, but it is also about being approachable and impartial for the good of all.
>
> (Primary teacher)

> A good leader is part of a group and moves with it – not necessarily always taking the lead. Leadership is about vision,

having some idea of what the establishment will look like in the future. Leadership also involves the ethos of the school – what the school stands for. It is about using the skills of the staff and developing what is there.

(Primary teacher)

The teachers were clear that leadership was not the sole responsibility of the headteacher. They had clearly taken on board the need for themselves and colleagues to take on some area of responsibility and a leadership role within the school:

Leadership is about vision, direction, inspiration, motivation and ethos – but the head need not be the leader in all of these – a large school needs other good leaders.

(Secondary teacher)

Management, in comparison with leadership, was more concerned with setting up systems and administering them:

Management is about structures and the smooth and effective running of the school.

(Primary teacher)

Management is about creating and maintaining the administrative systems/structures needed to achieve the direction and vision.

(Secondary teacher)

A good leader has vision whereas a good manager has organization for the establishment.

(Primary teacher)

Although the teachers made this conceptual distinction between leadership and management they recognized that practically the two areas of activity were linked, especially in the case of headteachers. For example, a number of the teachers commented approvingly on the fact that the smooth running of the school was not interrupted by the absence of the headteachers: 'The school runs like clockwork whether the head is here or not' (Primary teacher). This meant that for teachers, management became an aspect of leadership, in that the ability to delegate management responsibilities and roles was a function of leadership: 'Others should do the day-to-day running of the school leaving the head free to lead' (Secondary teacher).

The practical implications of management on the lives of teachers meant they did not readily separate their judgement of headteachers as leaders or managers. They were, though, able to distinguish between the different skills, understandings and attributes each required and how well their headteacher fared in each area.

The fairly traditional images of leaders and leadership provided by teachers did not seem to reflect the radical changes in the role of the headteacher in the recent past. The fact that changes to the leadership demands made on headteachers were not reflected within the broad images used by the teachers was partially because these images contained aspects of leadership which appeared to be constants even within changing times: foresight, bravery, care, vision, etc. The impact of these changes was most discernible to the teachers in the means by which headteachers demonstrated their leadership in terms of their personal knowledge of staff and students; the support for the continuing professional development of staff; establishing and communicating a shared commitment to common values, ideals and standards; and being a fair but tough decision maker.

The person in the professional

The relationships between headteachers and teachers were particularly complicated because they were so multifaceted. The headteacher could be, and often was, part employer, part personnel officer, part role model, part friend, partly to be admired and partly to be resented. The teachers' accounts stressed the role their professional, and in some cases personal, relationships with the headteachers played in establishing them as leaders:

> The door is always open. You can come and talk about anything in your life . . . Whether it's your hobby . . . or a concern with your family at home or if it is a problem in the classroom or if a child is worrying you or someone's parent . . . He has time for you.
>
> (Primary teacher)

She seems to know all about us and is always there to talk if we need to. A shoulder to cry on and a sound guide and friend, she's always there for staff and pupils 24 hours a day. I don't mean she's a saint, just a good human being.

(Infant teacher)

Strong personality . . . Big personality . . . He gets to know the teachers . . . Socially . . . To know who they are . . . If you respect them, they'll respect you.

(Primary teacher)

Many of these relationships were based around the headteacher modelling particular ways of working:

He's a perfectionist, professional. He likes everything to be right. He sets high standards for himself.

(Primary teacher)

and building mutual trust and respect:

He supports the staff and shows that their contribution is valued so that in return the staff are willing to support him in difficult times.

(Primary teacher)

What constituted an effective relationship between a teacher and a headteacher changed as both of their careers developed, and as the needs of their school changed. The kind of relationship which was appropriate, or achievable, for a headteacher to establish with a newly qualified teacher (NQT) was very different within a couple of years. Particularly, once the NQT had developed as a teacher and member of the school community:

In the first few years you are afraid of the head . . . If he walks through when you're teaching you have to be doing what's right . . . As the years have worn by he's become more of a friend . . . He's really concerned with your personal life as well. How it affects you. So if you have a trauma, he supports you to the hilt. He knows when to draw the line . . . A mixture of support and guidance.

(Primary teacher)

Similarly, new headteachers' relationships with their staff differed from those of established heads. There was an important period of establishing themselves as the 'head' and becoming part of the school culture. Coping, anticipating and managing the dynamics of these relationships was the mark of an effective leader from the teachers' perspective. The sheer number and complexity of these relationships often meant that headteachers had to prioritize certain elements of them or even delegate them to others:

> He's got more distant. He's taken on more responsibilities outside school. He's moved further away from the day-to-day running of the school, although he does know what's going on . . . He finds out from the people below what's going on.
>
> (Primary teacher)

The teachers involved in these relationships were individuals who, like headteachers, had invested a great deal of their lives and personal energies in their schools, who had their own sense of professionalism, often marked by a high degree of individualism and autonomy, and who judged headteachers from a number of perspectives:

> The head makes staff feel valued and worthwhile and trusted to get on with the job. He knows when to leave people alone and what they need.
>
> (Secondary teacher)

The teachers also recognized tensions not only in their own relationships with the headteacher but also in those of other colleagues:

> He doesn't like to say 'No'. He is almost 'too nice' and perhaps gives false expectations at times.
>
> (Secondary teacher)

> As a head he is now accountable to so many people that he can't ever please all of them all of the time, which he finds stressful.
>
> (Primary teacher)

Teachers valued their headteachers' ability to develop good relationships with students, almost as much as their own relationships with them. Recognizing that headteachers were ex-classroom teachers, they expected them to exhibit the kinds of professional norms and expectations they themselves aspired to in working with students:

He is aware of the problems children have and is supportive of the needs of individual pupils.

(Primary teacher)

He is involved with the pupils in a very human way through his teaching and through his turn on dinner and 'bus duty'.

(Secondary teacher)

Establishing and communicating a shared commitment to common values, ideals and standards

Values and vision

The teachers, like many of the other groups interviewed, were aware that headteachers as leaders needed to provide some kind of coherent view of the school and how it should develop and, overwhelmingly, they respected these 'visions':

He would have a school full of really independent learning children . . . who are really co-operative . . . where you could walk into a classroom and you would see every child doing different things . . . He likes the family atmosphere.

(Primary teacher)

As visions these statements were relatively unthreatening to most staff and appealed to the value frameworks and beliefs of many of the teachers:

He provides child-centred leadership. The education, social development, security and well-being of the children are paramount.

(Primary teacher)

What seemed to count more in terms of how they were judged as leaders was less the acceptability of their vision than how well they implemented it, how well they were able to build some form of common commitments, form cohesive groups within the school and bring them together:

The head is very good at seeing the school as a whole rather than as little bits of interaction. She has a good overview of the organization and knows how to get the most from everyone here.

(Primary teacher)

Easy going and will allow other people to do things. Doesn't save it all for himself. Is not looking for all the accolades. He doesn't want everything to be his idea, which some people have a problem with. He's not bothered where the ideas come from. Space to develop their ideas but of course we are not all going off at a tangent. The job of the head is to know what is going on in each bit. Not so much actually being the leader of the project . . . The head is a co-ordinator as well as co-ordinating outside.

(Special school teacher)

She has a holistic approach to pupils and staff.

(Primary teacher)

To her everyone is valued because she believes that if all have a sense of their own self-worth they will do their best.

(Primary teacher)

In shaping the development of the school, headteachers gained their credibility as leaders both for achieving shared commitment to their 'vision' or 'strategic thinking' and for the degree of care with which they nurtured the 'living organism' of the school:

The head is a nurturer rather than an organizer. She wraps her arms around the school and guides it forward. She is not a strategic planner but is someone who knows how the lifeblood of the school ebbs and flows.

(Infant teacher)

or dealt with the micro-political battles of everyday staffroom manoeuvring:

Although we can work closely there has to be a time when decisions are taken and she has to say whether we can or cannot do this . . . There has to be an ultimate authority where she sees the overall pattern.

(Primary teacher)

This is not a democracy. The head takes soundings not votes.

(Secondary teacher)

He's a good mediator.

> (Secondary teacher)

Continuing professional development

The headteachers' roles in staff development were a key avenue for demonstrating their leadership:

> She gets satisfaction from seeing staff make progress and develop. She pushes staff forward and encourages them to go on to bigger and better things.
>
> (Primary teacher)

> All the time the head gives a lot of support for my own development, really praising where praise is due.
>
> (Primary teacher)

The focus, though, was not just on teachers as individuals but on their contribution to the school as a whole, and the role they played in improving the quality of education on offer:

> She has a responsibility towards the teachers in terms of she needs to ensure that they are doing what the children are here to achieve. She has to ensure that we are doing our job properly.
>
> (Infant teacher)

Staff development, therefore, played a key role in developing the kind of culture that headteachers wanted to engender. Here one teacher reflects on what might be called the 'learning culture' in their school:

> Here there is pride in work, co-operating, learning and growing as a teacher, and believing your work is important.
>
> (Secondary teacher)

Staff development was welcomed by teachers and viewed as a means of rewarding staff, remotivating others, and at times keeping busy those who need to be occupied:

> He allowed me as an NQT [newly qualified teacher] to get established and trusted me to ask for help if I needed it. For my part I feel that I could ask for help and get it. He provides resources for staff development which shows that he values this as a professional activity.
>
> (Primary teacher)

He believes in giving opportunities for people to achieve.

(Primary teacher)

There's a lot of in-house development and if somebody wants to attend a training course they are supported. The ones that do well, he pushes them, encourages them. If you want to do well he will push you.

(Primary teacher)

Being a fair and tough decision maker

Leadership has always been expressed through the ability to make the 'tough' decision. Although the nature of these decisions seemed to be constantly changing, there was a sense that issues were dealt with fairly:

The head doesn't have favourites, she treats everyone equally. You get a sense that she is keen to demonstrate that she is unbiased and fair in her decision making and leadership.

(Secondary teacher)

He has a strong sense of fairness.

(Secondary teacher)

I have never worked with a head who demonstrates integrity and love at the same time. She lives by her core values and demonstrates them in her everyday work.

(Infant teacher)

I think she is very aware of what is going on through monitoring systems of teacher quality, pupils' work, parent opinions. I do think she is very aware.

(Infant teacher)

Metaphors

The metaphors that teachers used illustrated both the strategic and organizational elements of leadership and management. Therefore headteachers were sometimes 'skippers', 'captains', and 'mavericks':

He's the skipper, he keeps things ticking on the way he wants to. He helps with his friendly attitude ... He's got the 'fun' aspect ... It's enjoyable to walk through the door and have a nice smile. A nice greeting ... You don't think, 'Well if I bump into him he's going to grab me for something.'

(Primary teacher)

Definitely a maverick, basically, he'll get what he wants ... whether it is teaching, staffing, anything to do with material resources ... He'll find a way by hook or by crook ... For the good of the school and the good of the children.

(Primary teacher)

They were also 'jugglers' keeping various balls in the air, the 'core of the reactor', 'the rock' and the 'spider at the centre of a web' keeping an eye on everything:

I see her as a bit of a juggler. She's one of those jugglers who doesn't like to drop any balls. She's constantly got more balls in the air than she can manage at once. But she gets quite stressed when one of those balls drop and occasionally they do.

(Infant teacher)

A big spider in the middle of the web, and he runs out here and there.

(Special school teacher)

Conclusion

The teachers' perspectives, like those of other groups we interviewed, recognized the demands and tensions of the job. In tone they fell between the critical insights offered by deputy headteachers who saw the workings of the headteacher at very close quarters and the more distant perceptions of much of the wider school community. They were the comments of those who not only recognized the power of the headteacher to affect their own individual professional lives but also the whole nature of the school and its culture. They were, therefore, tinged occasionally with resentment on an individual level, if their own hopes and ideas had been thwarted, but also admiration for the qualities of those carrying out a difficult job.

5

THE PERSPECTIVES OF GOVERNORS, PARENTS AND SUPPORT STAFF

Since the beginning of the 1980s, successive governments have sought to increase the accountability of schools, in part by increasing the responsibilities of governing bodies. This has meant that many governors, in particular chairs of governors, have had to acquire a substantial knowledge of how schools are run. For example, a recent study exploring the relationship between inspection and school improvement suggests that 'in many cases inspection has been beneficial because it has forced a governing body to become formally involved and to be called into account' (Earley 1998: 35). Heads are often instrumental in helping governors to understand and interpret much of this information, and are also the main source of intelligence about what is happening in the school. This has meant that many governors often have a close working relationship with their headteacher. Where this closeness has existed, the effectiveness of the governing body has been enhanced: 'All the research into governing bodies agreed that the crucial factor in its [sic] effectiveness is the attitude of the head' (Earley 1998: 33). Governors meet the headteacher during monitoring visits as well as on more formal occasions like governors' meetings. The chair of governors is invariably the first to be consulted by the head in a crisis and, indeed, in any decision making involving the day-to-day running of the school.

Parents also often have a close relationship with the school. Many visit the school on a regular basis. Parents of primary schoolchildren, for example, may drop off and collect their children from school every day. Most schools support a programme of regular open evenings and consultation sessions. Parents and governors are recipients of newsletters, often written by the headteacher. Many parents and governors are in a position to act as 'participant observers', and both groups can provide interesting perspectives on leadership which are different from, and therefore complementary to, those offered by other stakeholders.

Support staff see their heads fulfilling a number of functions which are essential to the efficient running of the school, but which are usually peripheral to the teaching and learning of students. In that respect they provide a different perspective to those of teachers and students. School secretarial staff, for example, invariably have an executive function which involves them in an intimate, one-to-one relationship with the headteacher. They, perhaps more than anyone else in the school, are aware of the various pressures which the head faces on a daily basis. They are often, particularly in primary schools, an important part of the filtration process of access to the head. Secretaries are more aware than others of the volume of communications (spoken, written and now electronic) passing in and out of schools. It is hardly surprising that the school secretary is often one of the prime confidantes of the headteacher.

School keepers, caretakers and premises officers also often enjoy a close managerial relationship with their headteachers. They are often the first to see them in the morning, and the last to see them when they lock the school up for the evening. They are keenly aware of the amount of time individual heads spend at work. They also see the heads as crisis managers, dealing with cases of vandalism and accidental damage to the premises. School keepers, like other support staff, may have had experience of employment outside education which enables them to make comparisons between their heads and other managers.

Leadership and management

In general, both parents and governors were able to distinguish clearly between leadership and management, while at the same time recognizing that the two were inextricably linked in the role fulfilled by headteachers. As the chair of governors of a primary school, who herself had management experience, put it: 'Ideally the two dovetail: leadership is about having vision – the ability to look ahead. Management is more to do with the day-to-day running of the school.' A secondary school chair made a similar point:

> Leadership and management are interlinked – you can't really have one without the other. Leadership is about developing other people, setting an example and setting standards for others to develop further. Management is more about systems – how you work with staff and pupils. It is about ways of achieving where you are going.

Although among parents there was a recognition that management responsibilities could be delegated to others, they identified the headteacher as the main provider of leadership – the symbolic 'figurehead' role:

> Management can be delegated by the head to the staff, governors and parents, but there must be one person who is the leader or figurehead, and that is the head.
>
> (Primary parent)

As vital actors in the day-to-day administration of the school, support staff were unsurprisingly voluble about the management functions of their headteachers. They, too, were aware of the role of the head as figurehead both in the school and within the larger community:

> I've always thought of [the head] as a figurehead more than anything else. He is the last resort. If anyone needs a good telling off, he'll give it to them.
>
> (Secondary classroom assistant)

The potential remoteness of this role seemed to be tempered by an awareness among support staff that heads felt a sense of ownership and personal pride for the school, and that it was this sense of pride which helped motivate them:

> He's very proud of the school.
>
> (Primary school keeper)

> She's very proud of the school, and she loves it when parents
> want their children to come to the school.
>
> (Primary support staff)

This echoes the primary headteacher who felt she was showing
people around her own house when conducting visitors around
her school.

Support staff also detected a certain relentlessness in their heads
in getting things done:

> He seems to get what he wants . . . He doesn't take no for
> an answer very easily.
>
> (Primary school secretary)

> He does seem to get what he wants . . . He's got this
> ability . . .
>
> (Primary support staff, same school)

This was seen as a function of their organizational ability:

> [The head] is very organized. She is very strong on getting
> the documentation right. She knows we have got time pres-
> sures but she does want it done, and it does have to be
> done . . .
>
> (Secondary support staff)

their enthusiasm:

> She shows enthusiasm, and hopes others will be enthusiastic
> . . .
>
> (Primary midday supervisor)

and of a toughness of character which other stakeholders, like
teachers, had also acknowledged:

> She is a good leader. She is diplomatic and yet she is strong.
> It is that combination of strength and determination as well
> as diplomacy that carries her through.
>
> (Secondary classroom assistant)

Support staff also recognized a range of interpersonal skills
and strategies employed by their heads in their determination to
get things done. The first was the ability of the various heads,
particularly but not exclusively primary heads, to instil a sense
of teamwork in their schools:

She makes us feel we are part of a team. We're all cogs in a wheel . . . make the school do what it does, and be as good as it is . . .

> (Primary school secretary)

We all pull together . . . We are a friendly school.

> (Primary support staff)

This sense of teamwork was often promoted through strategies which built upon personal loyalty to the head:

He gives everyone a place, therefore the individual is part of the whole, giving the school a community feel.

> (Secondary support staff)

He makes everyone feel that they are important, and that they have a worthwhile contribution to make. He writes thank you letters to all who have helped, for example with a concert, the next morning.

> (Support staff, same school)

From these comments it would appear that staff did their jobs well as much to please their respective heads as to fulfil their contractual obligations. Heads seemed to spend a lot of time and energy on building up such loyalty, and it often meant that they had created a sense of informality and even intimacy in their relations with their support staff. Support staff seemed, for example, to be more aware than other members of the school community of the personal costs of being a head:

She switches off in a very controlled way – she has to stop at a certain point, otherwise she would 'pop'. She often just goes round the school at that point. She's never been off sick – her job satisfaction seems to carry her through.

> (Primary support staff)

The ability to 'recharge' themselves was carefully observed:

She wanders around the school with purpose, and renews herself.

> (Primary general assistant)

A pupil drowned in the swimming pool. He found it diffi-cult to cope with on a personal level . . . He held himself personally responsible . . . Through reassuring others he reassured himself . . .

(Secondary premises officer)

A sense of humour was an essential part of a head's demeanour:

The job is stressful because there is a lot to cope with, but he has a good sense of humour which seems to get him through.

(Secondary support staff)

These examples showed a willingness on the part of heads to share quite personal details of their public and private lives with their support staff. The ability to combine drive and determination with an overt humanity, bordering on fragility, seemed to be a feature of many of the heads in this study.

In common with other groups in the school community, support staff recognized that their heads were good communicators:

She's a communicator . . . easy to talk to . . . easy to get on with . . .

(Primary school secretary)

The ability of heads to accommodate the diverse nature of the school community was implicit in their comments:

I think to be able to lead you've obviously got to be able to communicate. I think [the head] is someone who is able to get on with all types of people, and I think that makes for good leadership. He is approachable . . . He can get the message across.

(Secondary school secretary)

They need to be able to reach all levels . . . You are not always on the same level as the people you work with . . . So you need to be able to come down to certain things, to be able to discuss things with people. So they have to be agile in the way they speak to people, and not let people feel undermined by the terminology they use . . . [They] must also be able to cope with the obviously top-of-the-range people they have to deal with.

(Secondary classroom assistant)

Like the teachers in our featured schools, support staff highlighted the heads' recognition of the power of delegation, particularly in terms of the perceived self-value which it instilled in others:

> She seeks the best way from experts, and seeks opinions. She likes new ideas.
>
> (Primary school keeper)

> [The head] is a good delegator. He is able to give people responsibility, and allow them to get on and do the job.
>
> (Secondary school secretary)

The support staff in the featured schools thus saw leadership and management as a combination of decisiveness and humanity. Heads who spent time on developing relationships with those they managed seemed likely to instil a personal loyalty and the personal following necessary to make the running of the school a team effort, rather than being dependent upon a hierarchical management structure or the work of a few individuals. Being at the receiving end of the head's leadership and management, the support staff interviewed were able to give a richer and more intimate perspective of their heads' activities than governors and parents.

Organizational management

Parents and governors identified two main issues with regard to the management of staff by headteachers. First, they saw the value of staff having a clear sense of purpose and pulling together to achieve common goals. The following statement by a parent governor of a primary school illustrates this point:

> She was heavily involved in getting the staff together and ensuring that they knew what they were supposed to be doing, and what it meant to the school, not only for now but for the future of the school . . .
>
> (Primary parent governor)

Second, parents and governors recognized the importance of treating the staff as professionals by the degree of autonomy they were granted, the delegation of responsibility to them and the opportunities they were given to further their professional development. The following comments of a primary chair of governors echo many such appreciative ones made by teachers and support staff in other schools in this study:

> His greatest achievement is the way he has pulled the staff and the school together. He has given the staff the freedom to act, and has delegated responsibilities to them. He has enabled staff to develop professionally through further study.
>
> (Primary chair of governors)

The energy and expertise of the head of a large comprehensive school was recognized by a chair of governors with a wide experience in the private sector at a senior level:

> You cannot relate the jobs people do to the salary they get – money is not the key motivator in a school. If pay was related to performance the head of this school should get twice his present salary.
>
> (Secondary chair of governors)

Beyond consultation by the head on technical aspects of their job, support staff seemed to be involved primarily in policy implementation rather than policy making. This confirms research findings elsewhere (MacGilchrist *et al.* 1995). Heads were therefore observed as action-oriented decision makers rather than as partners in a decision-making process:

> She sees to any problems or needs immediately.
>
> (Primary support staff)

> He looks trouble straight in the eye.
>
> (Primary school secretary)

This element of autocracy in the schools' decision-making processes was not resented by support staff. Indeed, there was a sense of admiration which was often conveyed in their comments:

> He makes the decisions and he stands by them. We may not like the decisions all the time but he's made them, and that's it. He does have to make some pretty grotty decisions sometimes, but they do have to be made . . .
>
> (Secondary support staff)

While the changes were taking place there were lots of decisions that were actually made like that [snaps fingers], and they had to be made and they had to be done, and they were acted upon.

(Support staff, same school)

Members of the support staff who were involved in the administration of the school's budget testified as to the financial expertise of the heads, both in terms of administrative ability:

> She's good at shuffling the money – deciding what to buy and knowing those who are going to be affected by her decisions . . .

(Primary administrative officer)

> He has his finger on the pulse of financial things – a very deep knowledge.

(Secondary finance officer)

and, in one of the featured secondary schools, of entrepreneurial flair:

> He is good at pushing for things – Technology status, the sixth form building, and now a sports complex.

(Secondary classroom assistant)

Within this culture of often autocratic decision making, the heads did not lose sight of the importance of the development of all staff. A number of the schools were involved in the 'Investors In People' initiative. While maintaining a focus upon servicing the education of the school's students, heads seemed to be able to communicate to support staff the worth and value of their own professional growth:

> She provided me with guidance when I was new to the job – she explains things in layman's terms.

(Primary administrative officer)

> She's hot on training and staff development.

(Finance officer, same school)

Ambition for others to progress, a feature of heads' attitudes towards the development of their students and teachers, extended to other groups in the school:

> Many [staff] have left for higher positions in other schools, and new teachers are quickly integrated – the head enables this to happen.

(Caretaker, same school)

She has made us more responsible for what we do in
midday supervision. She's encouraged supervisors to have
first-aid training. She encourages people to develop. She
encourages us to go for jobs.

(Primary midday supervisor)

Like some of the teachers interviewed, many of the parents,
governors and support staff recognized that headteachers did not
necessarily employ democratic methods in arriving at critical decisions relating to the running of their schools. What was recognized
was the acknowledgement by heads of the expertise of their staff,
their willingness to grant staff a degree of autonomy within their
various spheres of activity and the investment of time and resources in improving staff performance and career prospects.

The person in the professional

There was universal agreement among parents and governors
that all of the headteachers in the sample worked extremely
hard for the good of their schools, the following statement by a
governor being typical:

The head is amazing. She works very long hours. She is there
first thing and last thing. I think she sleeps at the school
sometimes.

(Infant governor)

The view was confirmed by a parent at the same school, who
also drew attention to the positive attitude and demeanour which
accompanied the hard work:

I think the head works very hard, although she is always
cheerful and friendly.

(Parent, same school)

However, in the case of some of the heads in the sample, their
attempts to reconcile the conflicting demands of being both a
teacher and the head of a school were seen as a source of pressure and stress:

Being a teacher as well puts her under a lot of pressure
. . . having to teach and have time off to run the school is
very hard.

(Primary parent)

Attention was sometimes drawn to the perceived isolation of the headteacher as a potential source of stress:

> Issues can be shared, but at the end of the day responsibility rests with the head.
>
> (Primary parent)

For their part, governors showed themselves to be especially aware of the demands imposed on headteachers (and their colleagues) by Ofsted inspections:

> The Ofsted inspection got to a lot of the staff so much that many were ill afterwards, but the head stayed calm and provided strong leadership throughout.
>
> (Primary chair of governors)

Similarly, governors provided an insight into the cumulative effect which managing change in schools over a period of time could have on hardworking and dedicated headteachers:

> His health has suffered in times of stress – the strain has shown in the last eighteen months. Problems can be shared with the governing body and with senior staff, but he is dedicated and, despite advice, he won't take time off school.
>
> (Secondary governor)

However, it was suggested that for some headteachers the pressure of meeting the challenges of the job gave them the greatest satisfaction:

> He enjoys both the challenge of the job and the 'buzz' he gets from doing it.
>
> (Primary chair of governors)

The parents placed high value on headteachers being available to them for personal contacts, and schools being sufficiently open and accessible to parents that they had a sense that home and school are working in partnership with each other:

> You feel that you are welcome . . . the liaison between parents and teachers on how the children are progressing . . . the work you are invited to come and look at . . . all the concerts and productions. . . . You don't feel as though you are an outsider . . . It's not an 'us and them' situation. It's working as a team.
>
> (Primary parent)

I think that they have got to be approachable. Parents are more involved with their children's education nowadays . . . and therefore they want answers to their queries, and they want guidance when things start going wrong.

(Primary parent)

An important element in the open access to schools which parents valued was the willingness of headteachers to show that they were taking them seriously by listening to what they had to say. Parents are often at the end of a long line of involvement with schools and other public services. Consequently, they find the willingness of a headteacher to listen, and the ability to respond, to be highly supportive:

It's just nice to be taken seriously as a parent . . . In the past with another headteacher I felt it was going in one ear and out of the other.

(Primary parent)

For their part, governors indicated that they too regarded it as important that their headteachers were accessible to people with problems, and recognized that operating such an 'open-door' policy could only be achieved at some personal cost to the head concerned:

He is sympathetic, finding time for others with problems, even if it means working long hours outside school time, and his door is always open.

(Primary chair of governors)

Finally, parents stressed the importance to them of headteachers spending time away from their administrative responsibilities in order to gather intelligence from around the school, and to be seen to be doing so:

She's overburdened with admin. She could be buried in it and office-bound, but she handles it well and is still seen around the school and in classrooms. She has a sense of what is going on, keeps her ear to the ground and maintains a high profile round the school.

(Primary parent)

The priority given by heads to building relationships with other members of their school community was also closely observed and noted by the support staff. Administrative staff noted the hard work involved:

> He tends to get rid of all his paperwork by coming in early in the morning so he's got his day to be where he's needed . . . He gets to know all his staff and the children as well.
>
> (Primary school secretary)

The attention to detail of the various heads was also highlighted:

> She remembers all the pupils' names, and she's concerned for people. She tries to keep in touch with parents . . .
>
> (Primary support staff)

> He sent flowers to a sick caretaker.
>
> (Secondary premises officer)

A number of the staff recognized the motivational effect that such interest and concern had had upon them:

> If she asked me to work all weekend for no extra pay, I would because she asked me.
>
> (Primary support staff)

> I work 48 hours for him for 37 hours' pay.
>
> (Secondary administrator)

As well as being proactive in developing relationships, heads were also admired by support staff, as they were by most members of their school communities, for their availability and approachability:

> People can go with their personal problems to the head – she does not detach herself from people.
>
> (Primary administrative assistant)

> He is always approachable all the time. The door is always open to deal with people – teachers, everybody.
>
> (Secondary support staff)

Support staff, many of whom had personal contact with the head on a daily basis, were well aware of the tensions often implicit in sustaining friendships and getting things done:

We have our ups and downs.

(Primary school keeper)

He finds it hard to please everyone.

(Meals supervisor, same school)

The tensions for this head often led to a degree of visible stress:

He feels pretty low at times, for example if he feels that personal criticism of him by the staff is unjust.

(Secondary support staff)

While support staff were generally not present at the main policy- and decision-making meetings in the schools, heads apparently compensated for this absence by consulting them informally on technical issues related to their jobs, and by showing an overt concern for their well-being and professional development. Hence, what could be categorized as a 'formal' style of management, where heads brought to support staff the aims, goals and decisions negotiated elsewhere for them to implement (Bush 1986), was tempered by a concern on the part of the head about the impact of such decisions on those implementing the policies.

Governors and parents shared with the support staff of the schools an awareness and appreciation of the humanity, and indeed the vulnerability, of their headteachers. This was unsurprising. The heads in this study placed great importance upon the development of personal relationships with a wide range of members of their school community. They tried to make themselves available at all times, and they took trouble to gather information about people. Their jobs were difficult, time-consuming and stressful. In energetically maintaining ongoing relationships with individual students, teachers, secretaries, school keepers, parents and governors, it was difficult to mask or hide any stress. In being humane, our heads also showed themselves to be human.

Professional leadership

Presence and charisma were identified by parents and governors as being important ingredients in the professional leadership of schools provided by headteachers:

The head is charismatic, no doubt about it. Watch her in action and you'll soon see how her staff and the pupils worship her and find her totally engaging.

(Infant governor)

Parents and governors also recognized that the leadership which their headteacher provided reached beyond the school and out into the community:

The school is a community school – it is part of the way of life around here. The head is wonderful, she reaches out to the community and draws us close to the school.

(Secondary parent)

Parents and governors also revealed in their responses that they expected the headteachers of their schools to be both caring and tough-minded:

I expect somebody that is strong enough to cope with all the various pressures that are put upon them. I also want somebody that the children can respect and the parents can respect. I don't want children to be afraid of them. I think that there has to be an element of the caring/sharing thing . . .

(Secondary governor)

It was also evident from their responses that many parents looked to the headteacher and the school for both moral support and practical help at times when they were having problems with their children:

I trust the school implicitly. If they say something needs doing I wouldn't even think about questioning it. I'd say, 'Yes, OK, fine'. They've got experience of dealing with emotional and educational problems. They've got more experience of it than me; even though I'm [pupil's] mother they know what they are talking about.

(Special school parent)

Support staff were less inclined to comment on the educational leadership provided by the head, largely because few of them observed their heads in activities where they were fulfilling this function. Very few, for example, attended staff meetings, or were present during whole school assemblies. Parents and governors recognized the educational expertise which their heads possessed. Parents in particular valued the heads' knowledge of their own children, and their ability to apply their expertise in solving any problems their children might have.

Values and vision

It was evident that both parents and governors were able to identify the personal values which helped to inform the educational practice and views of headteachers:

> The ethos of the school shows that he values people of all ages and backgrounds. He believes that most people, including children, have good in them and that the school must work on developing their potential. His own Christian beliefs come through, inculcating in the pupils a tolerance for children and adults from other walks of life, including those from other cultures and religions.
>
> (Primary chair of governors)

A similar view was voiced by a parent who also highlighted a recurrent theme in the responses of parents and governors – the importance the headteachers attached to developing the potential of individual children:

> The head wants every child to achieve. He values every child's achievements. He values the opinions of parents. His values are humanist more than Christian.
>
> (Secondary parent)

This concern for the development of individual pupils was illustrated by the importance which some headteachers placed upon the children enjoying their experience of school:

> She is caring, strong on setting high standards for the youngsters of every age. The aim is that, whatever their level of ability, they should do their very best. There is a sense of fun and enjoyment here as well.
>
> (Primary governor)

The head believes that the school should aim to develop in pupils a respect for themselves and for others, and that if children have potential in any area it is the head's job to draw it out and develop it . . . He also believes that the school should provide good supportive pastoral care, especially for those children who lack support at home.

(Secondary governor)

The headteachers in the sample were also regarded by both the parents and governors questioned as having high moral standards and high levels of personal integrity, which were reflected in their professional behaviour:

The head is an honest person who sometimes makes mistakes, but who will always admit to them.

(Primary governor)

The head is an excellent communicator who judges every situation and case on its merits. She is above all fair in her management of the school.

(Secondary governor)

Finally, it was evident from what was said by both governors and parents that many headteachers found time to get to know the children, and enjoyed their interactions with them and their parents:

Teaching to her is her vocation, a calling . . . She believes in being close to people . . . To her, children and their parents matter . . . She probably knows all the children – their names, quirks and achievements. They all speak to her, and smile.

(Primary chair of governors)

The head is wonderful with children. They are obviously the most important people in the school; always have been, from day one. She treats them as individuals, as people in their own right . . . They know where they stand with her.

(Primary chair of governors)

Views from support staff about their headteachers' vision for the school tended to be fragmented, and related to their own particular job. This is unsurprising. Most support staff were not present at the public occasions when such visions were articulated – meetings of teachers, open evenings, parents' evenings. Hence support staff were dependent upon their own daily contact with headteachers in arriving at their views. Some were aware, however, of the primacy given to the well-being and achievement of students in the school:

She wants every child to achieve their full potential, and she makes sure that the staff do their best to get the pupils to achieve their best.

                              (Primary support staff)

The children do very much come first . . .

                              (Secondary classroom assistant)

A secretary in a primary school observed her head dealing on a daily basis with student discipline:

She certainly likes discipline. She is concerned that children do obey the rules. On the bullying question, she does take time with children . . .

A secondary caretaker derived his head's general views on education from his attitudes on the state of the school:

He is a traditionalist – tidiness, cleanliness . . . He likes the school neat, clean and clear of graffiti and litter.

Other staff made similar extrapolations from the expectations expressed to them by their heads about their job performance:

She believes in very high standards throughout the school.

                              (Primary support staff)

Support staff expressed their appreciation of heads who were sensitive to issues of status within the school, and who valued the contribution they made to the running of the school:

She values everyone's viewpoint.

                              (Primary support staff)

He treats everybody from the dustman to the member of staff with regard, and I think not everybody has that quality in his position. He gives them confidence in themselves.

                              (Primary school secretary)

The heads seemed able to maintain a balance within their relationships with support staff between the personal, acknowledged above as an element in their development of teamwork in the school, and the professional: the active deployment of staff to secure the goals of the school. Although the heads showed their staff a human and often vulnerable side to their natures, they were apparently able to maintain throughout the vicissitudes of the school day a consistent demeanour:

She never shows signs of not being able to cope. At the time of the Ofsted inspection she gave out an air of calm, and handled it all very well. She was very supportive of the staff at this and other times when they were under stress.

(Primary administrative officer)

He acknowledges a job well done, and has a personal touch. He is tough, consistent and persistent!

(Secondary support staff)

This combination of caring, humanity and respect for others inspired both loyalty and what almost amounted to awe in some support staff:

Whatever he's had to do, he inspires it in other people to do it.

(Primary support staff)

He leads by example all the way.

(Secondary support staff)

Support staff also observed from close quarters the hard work which the heads put into their job:

She turns up here early in the morning and leaves late at night. She works long hours and puts in extra time at governors' and other meetings.

(Primary caretaker)

In other situations the work of the head would be done by four or five different people.

(Administrative officer, same school)

This work ethic often translated into similar expectations of others (something recognized by the students in some of the featured schools):

He expects hard work from all – he provides a good model.

(Secondary support staff)

Governors, parents and support staff all viewed their heads as highly moral and ethical individuals who gave priority to the interests of students. They shared this view with other stakeholder groups, although the perception was less well developed in the students themselves, perhaps because they were less aware of the nature of the variety of relationships in which their heads found themselves.

The equal regard shown by heads for all their staff effectively restored a democratic element to a working relationship which largely excluded one side from the major decision-making processes within the school. By treating support staff as equals, or indeed superiors, in their realms of competence, and by giving praise when appropriate, heads gained the respect and further consolidated the loyalty of their workforce.

Strategic leadership

The strategic leadership role exercised by headteachers in helping governors and staff to come to terms with externally generated changes enabled the school to keep 'ahead of the game'. This was widely acknowledged by those questioned, especially by governors:

> She works hard (for example she is in school late in the evenings and during the holidays, and takes work home) to keep up to speed and up-to-date with all the information, so that she can be ahead of the game and can keep us [the governors] informed, and cascade information to the staff.
> (Primary chair of governors)

It was also recognized by governors that, at a time of rapid change, headteachers needed to exercise critical judgements about potential innovations:

> He is always looking for improvements – but *not* change for change's sake.
> (Secondary chair of governors)

The responses of school governors also offered interesting insights into the way in which some headteachers engaged them in dialogue as 'critical friends' about educational issues as part of the decision-making process:

> Most of the parent governors see her as a friend as well as a headteacher – somebody that you can talk to, that you can air your differences with . . . What is good about her is that she may not always like what you are saying but she does

listen, and will always come back to you with an argument
if she has got one. Same as you can go back to her and say
we don't think it is the right thing.

> (Secondary parent governor)

The financial constraints under which maintained schools
operated, and the urgent need for prudent financial management and entrepreneurial enterprise on the part of headteachers,
was another recurrent theme to emerge in discussion:

> The head has her finger on the pulse, and is very good at
> seeing the opportunity for getting more funding. The com-
> munity group pays a small sum of money every week, and
> every resource is recycled if possible.

> (Secondary governor)

Similarly, the ability of the head to maintain a clear sense of
purpose in the face of competing demands, and to have confidence to deal with those pressures, was identified by governors as
important to the organizational leadership of the school:

> There are constant pressures . . . as a result of externally gen-
> erated change, but he has never gone under – he has always
> known what he was doing. He has commitment and confid-
> ence in his beliefs. He thinks and then acts, and has the
> strength of his convictions.

> (Primary chair of governors)

The need for headteachers in the current climate of rapid
change to keep abreast of new developments (not least to be
able to keep staff and governors informed), to take responsibility
for their own continuing professional development and to network
with other heads, was widely recognized among the governors
questioned:

> He is continuously developing professionally, not through
> attending conferences but by translating reports for the
> governors to keep them informed. He also gets lots of support
> from other secondary school headteachers.

> (Secondary governor)

Finally, the ability of headteachers to take a strategic overview
of the school as a whole and to pull together different activities,
so that they worked with each other for the improvement of the
school, was widely acknowledged by governors:

He has an overview of everything. He gets everyone (staff, parents' association and others) to work to the common goal of high standards. He gets the business community to contribute, and parents help. The children's expectations of themselves are raised. By means of a massive number of different activities he has raised the standing of the school.

(Secondary governor)

Their head's ability to develop the culture of their schools in a context of increasing, externally driven demands was a critical element in the governance of the case study schools. It was clearly of prime importance to the governors of these schools. The heads were avid readers and good communicators, and were perceived by their governing bodies as exercising professional discretion. Their ability to provide an overview of what was happening in the school and to appraise new initiatives clearly made their governors' task easier, and kept the school 'ahead of the game'. Support staff had little to say about the ability of their heads to build and consolidate a particular culture in the school. Although they communicated with the heads on a daily basis, support staff conceded that theirs was a partial view of the school.

Metaphors

Both parents and governors experienced some difficulty when asked to suggest metaphors which would be appropriate to the leadership provided by their headteacher. One chair of governors, perhaps appreciating how much responsibility was delegated by the head to his colleagues at lower levels in the hierarchy, suggested:

The 'captain of the ship' is not adequate. Perhaps 'admiral of the fleet' would be more appropriate.

(Primary chair of governors)

A second chair of governors thought that perhaps a 'hospital matron' might be appropriate, but then went on to question its validity:

Because of the care and concern she shows, the 'matron' comes to mind. She does her 'rounds', but she listens in a way that is unlike a matron would do, and she's not feared like matrons once were.

(Primary chair of governors)

A parent who was in school on a regular basis as a classroom helper, and who was thus in a good position to observe the headteacher coping with a multiplicity of tasks simultaneously, suggested:

> She's a juggler (and a pretty good one on the whole), keeping many different balls in the air, and coping with the unpredictable.

(Primary parent)

Another parent emphasized a head's ability to lead both staff and pupils:

> He is the 'pied piper', controlling both the pupils and the staff.

(Secondary parent)

Finally, a governor speaking about the same headteacher identified his attributes before reaching a conclusion about what he considered to be an appropriate metaphor:

> He has warmth, rapport, a sense of humour, the ability to inspire others to develop with him. He loves his work, cares for people and has extra strength that comes from who knows where . . . It makes him unique – a real 'tower of strength' to the school.

(Governor, same school)

The metaphors of headship offered by support staff reflected the partial and often fragmented view of the head in action. The difficulty of reconciling different aspects of the head's job was often apparent in the pictures offered:

> He is a tiger with a sense of fun.

(Primary school keeper)

> I was thinking of a nun-type image, but then she's not at all nun-like. But in her way she is very calm with the children. Then she can be quite outrageous and very fun [sic].

(Secondary classroom assistant)

The directive function of the head was unsurprisingly high-lighted in many of those metaphors provided in other schools. In one primary school the head was 'captain of the ship', and 'grand master'. In another he was 'stage director'. Other metaphors focused on the team-building skills of the heads. One was seen as 'first among equals', 'the chief knitter' in a closely knit staff; another was 'team leader in control'. The most animated figure was provided by a primary school secretary, who saw her head as 'a flower opening up with the children'.

Conclusion

It was evident that the samples of parents and governors questioned enjoyed a close working relationship with their respective schools, and had a clear understanding of the personality and work of their headteachers. Overall, their responses suggested that they had a high regard for those headteachers who had a clarity of vision informed by clearly articulated personal values, and who were willing to direct their energies to improving the school from within and to helping pupils achieve their full potential. They also professed an admiration for headteachers whose values and beliefs were embodied in a range of behavioural characteristics which they could identify, including enthusiasm, commitment, hard work, honesty, integrity, support for others and a recognition of the worth of individuals. Their responses also attested to the ability of parents and governors to recognize the complexity and demands of the headteacher's role in the current context of rapid economic, social and educational change. In that respect, their views were often as perceptive as those of teachers in daily contact with their heads.

Support staff, by their very nomenclature, are important but peripheral to the main functions of a school, that is teaching and learning. Despite this, they echoed many of the views of their heads given by parents and governors, and indeed by teachers. The difference was that the views of support staff were firmly grounded in the employer–employee relationship they had with their headteachers. The heads shared the gift of making their support staff feel valued and respected. They did this by using strategies which often involved levels of informality and intimacy which could leave them looking vulnerable and fragile. Such was their gift, however, that support staff responded with respect rather than disdain to these shows of humanity. These unaffected personal relationships had a power to instil intense personal loyalty, and to produce work of a volume and quality above and beyond that required by contractual obligations.

6

THE STUDENTS'
PERSPECTIVES

A growing body of literature both here in the UK (Centre for Successful Schools 1990; Davies and Ellison 1995; Rudduck *et al.* 1996a, b; Maden and Rudduck 1997; Coleman and Collinge 1998; Cooper and Fielding 1998; Jackson *et al.* 1998) and overseas (Andersson 1996; Consortium on Chicago School Research 1996; Scottish CCC 1996; Wallace and Wildy 1996; Blum 1997; Osborn 1997; Restructuring Collaborative 1997) records students' views on how schools are run, and testifies to the value and authenticity of the student voice in providing information on how schools can improve. The worth of the student perspective has recently been recognized at the highest policy levels. Speaking at the national launch of the Children 5–16 Programme, comprising 22 overlapping ESRC projects designed to develop understanding of children's experience and participation in social institutions, Margaret Hewitt MP commented that 'there is much to learn in the shaping of policy from research with children' (quoted in James 1998). Not only can this voice be 'astute and articulate' (Smees and Thomas 1998), it can also cast a unique and distinctive light upon the school environment. At a recent international conference a Dutch student, following on from a Finnish head who had claimed to know everything about his own school, suggested that 'I see things you could never see' (quoted in MacBeath 1998).

It is not only the views of older students which have been canvassed on educational issues: primary school students have also been recent participants in such school-based research, on school ethos (Boyd and Reeves 1996), on reading habits (Beresford 1997), on working habits (Gipps and Tunstall 1997; Newman 1997; Flutter *et al.* 1998; Norwich 1998; Morgan and Morris 1999), and on the sources of student self-esteem (Meece and Miller 1996).

Almost all this literature on students' views is concerned with teaching and learning or with the school as a discrete social organization. There is very little written on students' views of headteachers and educational leadership. Reasons are not hard to find. Until quite recently students' voices have been 'lost voices' (Boyd and Jardine 1997). Studies of effective headship have tended to focus on areas in which students have tradition-ally had little say, for example curriculum development and administration. Students comprise a group who, by convention, expect to be managed and led in schools. The main quality generally required of students has been obedience (Levin 1994).

In England and Wales the main impetus behind the canvass-ing of students' views on their learning has been the increase in schools' public accountability through inspection and the pub-lication of test scores, and the subsequent desire to maximize students' learning outcomes. In this context 'what pupils say about teaching, learning and schooling is not only worth listen-ing to but provides an important foundation for thinking about ways of improving schools' (Rudduck *et al.* 1996a: 1).

Information was gathered from students in all but one of the schools. The ages of those interviewed ranged from Year 2 (6-year-olds) to Year 13 (18-year-olds). Heads were generally at pains to stress that, although students had been selected on the basis of their ability to communicate, they had not necessarily been chosen for their compliance. Information was collected in discussion groups ranging in size from four to ten, rather than through one-to-one interviews with students. In all cases the researchers departed from the main text of the questionnaire in order to concentrate more on specific aspects of the head's role as seen by the students – what heads did, what kind of people they were, students' perceptions of how they felt doing the job. Most groups, including the youngest, responded positively, exchanged views in an orderly and disciplined way, were encouraged to debate each other's ideas and were self-confident and articulate. The 'open-ended' nature of the questions asked meant that the researchers were 'facilitators' of a focus group rather than 'interrogators'. Consequently, interventions were kept to a minimum, and when they were made they were mainly to seek clarification or to redirect the discussion.

Leadership and management

Students of all ages recognized that heads had a different role from teachers in terms of the leadership and management of the school. Some were prepared to distinguish between the two functions:

> A leader tells people what to do. A manager organizes.
>
> (Year 6 student)

> He's mainly a leader – management doesn't impinge . . .
>
> (Year 13 student)

but generally the research team did not dwell on the distinction, with students tending to combine the two elements in their discussion of their respective heads.

Students identified five main components of the heads' role as leader and manager. Primary students in particular highlighted the strong element of direction of others in being a head:

> She tells teachers what to do.
>
> (Year 2 student)

> She bosses everybody about and makes everything organized.
>
> (Primary student)

Students of all ages recognized the element of personal responsibility attached to the job:

> Leadership is being responsible when things go wrong and feeling good if all goes well – being responsible for organizing everybody and being concerned for their welfare.
>
> (Primary student)

This responsibility extended to the welfare of students:

They have to look after you, if anything happens to you . . .
They can take a lot of responsibility.

(Primary student)

It also included responsibility for the daily running of the school:

Leadership involves being a trouble-shooter, sorting out the budget, making certain that the school is safe and secure for the pupils . . .

(Secondary student)

It was also universally recognized that such responsibilities could also involve making difficult decisions, decisions that might make the head unpopular with certain sections of the school:

Leadership involves making difficult decisions, like not allowing children outside to play when the weather is bad, and excluding a pupil for continued bad behaviour.

(Primary student)

To be the headteacher of this school must be really, really stressful because if things go wrong he must sort them out – the buck stops with him! If there is a personality clash between a teacher and the students, and the situation has reached stalemate, he has to make a judgement – and he's not always happy to have to do this.

(Secondary student)

The participation of others was another element recognized by students, including the youngest:

The people you're leading might get a bit jealous, feeling they were bossed about a bit. So you have to make them make decisions as well.

(Primary student)

He lets teachers do what they want to, up to a point.

(Year 6 student)

He's not bossy – he takes the advice of others.

(Year 9 student)

Finally, students recognized the element of ego fulfilment in being a head:

She has to have it her way.

(Primary student)

He has to be headteacher all the time – even at the 'Donkey Derby' he's still the head, even though it's more informal.
(Secondary student)

Students thus recognized that the job of being a head was multifaceted. What emerges starkly from this analysis, however, is a view that the exercise of the role could cause upset and tension within the school. There was some acknowledgement of the dilemmas implicit in being a head, dilemmas which were perhaps more readily recognized by the other groups in the school community that we interviewed: for example, that recognized by teachers and support staff of having to reconcile personal accountability with the desire to empower others, and of managing the often diverse needs of various stakeholder groups.

There was a clear awareness on the part of students of the micro-political context in which heads operated within their schools. This awareness was confirmed by a recognition of the contrasting emotions which heads could feel. Heads were apparently good in communicating their own sense of pride in the school's achievements, and the enjoyment of a job well done:

He enjoys teaching and working with the staff.
(Primary student)

Leadership is being honoured and proud to be head of the school.
(Secondary student)

He is proud of the improvements that have been made and happy with the pupils' achievements – not just academically but the good school teams, drama productions and music teaching.
(Secondary student)

There was, however, little surprise expressed when heads showed signs of feeling stress, although secondary heads were apparently better at hiding them than their primary colleagues:

A head is someone who is stressed but has a laugh sometimes and sometimes gets very angry.
(Primary student)

She shares her feelings at assemblies. She feeds off people smiling.
(Year 6 student)

She should have a break more often.

(Year 2 student)

Students' views of headteachers as leaders and managers reflected the variety of contexts in which heads were seen by students, and in which the work of heads was publicly discussed. Evidence from the interviews suggested that the students' distinctive perspective was derived from their daily experience as 'participant observers' of the social interactions which occurred in a wide range of the natural settings of school life – classrooms, corridors, assembly halls, headteacher's office, the playground – a wider range of settings than those experienced by the other groups interviewed in the study. Primary students in particular heard from a variety of sources, including teachers and parents, about the kind of activities undertaken by their headteachers. Heads were also observed by students at less frequent public occasions, for example at open evenings and social functions. Many students interviewed also encountered the head within the community, for example when shopping with their families. A number of the insights given suggested a high degree of personal contact between students and headteacher.

Students' perspectives thus encompassed a number of their own 'angles of observation', enabling them to offer valuable insights into the headteacher not merely as a leader and manager in the school, but as a teacher, a public figure and even as a private individual with a life beyond school.

Organizational management

Many of the heads featured in this study seemed to do much of their administrative work before and after school and so students had a fragmented view of the head's function of accomplishing the tasks of the organization. Students' encounters with their headteacher's administrative functions tended to be disparate and intermittent. There was a recognition, however, that heads undertook a wide variety of administrative tasks, and that many of them were demanding:

She keeps a lot in her head easily – despite having a great amount of work.

(Primary student)

She has got a lot on her mind, and she needs to be quite strict. She's good at making decisions.

(Primary student)

The key function of staff recruitment was acknowledged, often to quite a sophisticated degree:

She considers the staff she employs very carefully – she would *never* employ a teacher who did not like children, and she likes 'balanced teachers' (not those who are just 'all work' and nothing else).

(Primary student)

Teachers change a lot for various reasons, and it is often difficult to recruit teachers . . . That can lead to a disruption of learning.

(Secondary student)

There was a general awareness that there was a budget to be managed, although unsurprisingly there was a lack of clarity about the logistics of the process:

He counts the dinner money.

(Year 2 student)

He has to sort out a budget of over £4 million – and each member of staff has to get a fair share!

(Secondary student)

There was some appreciation of the financial decisions to be made:

She has to make difficult financial decisions, for example budgeting to pay for paper and buy other supplies such as expensive equipment for the SATs and to pay for making the school secure.

(Primary student)

Older students in one school showed some awareness of the entrepreneurial activity undertaken by their head. The following comment was typical of many:

His greatest achievement is getting Technology College status for the school.

(Year 9 student)

The featured heads were also seen as being good at making other decisions, particularly when sorting out people's problems. Referring to a previous head, a primary student commented that

> he never saw things through. He never really got cross. [The present head] can sort our problems out better. Behaviour is better now.
>
> (Year 6 student)

The critical nature of some of the decisions which heads had to make was also recognized:

> She has to make careful decisions, for example if a child is excluded for some reason it might attract bad publicity for the school, but if he or she is not excluded it could have a bad effect on the other children in the class.
>
> (Primary student)

> He is a wise, knowledgeable leader – he would know what to do in a crisis.
>
> (Year 6 student)

Students expressed appreciation where formal procedures had been put in place in order that their views could be canvassed:

> She likes listening to children, for example to the suggestions they make for improving the school at the School Council. There is a 'suggestions box' outside her office for sorting out problems.
>
> (Primary student)

Students unsurprisingly then had a less developed view, when compared to that of other members of the school community, of the role of the headteacher in the day-to-day running of the school. There is some awareness of the importance the heads in the study attached to staff recruitment, but little overt acknowledgement in any of the student responses of functions highlighted by other groups interviewed, and by the heads themselves – the monitoring of process and performance in the school, the professional development of the school staff, and the involvement of the school in the community. For students, much of the head's organizational management took place invisibly.

The person in the professional

One of the key factors identified as cementing student commitment to the process of learning is a meaningful, or 'authentic', relationship with an adult working at the school (Marzano *et al.* 1992; Gray and Wilcox 1995; Hopkins *et al.* 1997b, 1998). The nature of this relationship is such that it is normally provided by an individual teacher (Wallace 1996):

> The most enabling quality that one person can display to another is unconditional positive regard, a phrase which describes the clear, non-possessive, non-manipulative attitude which seeks the growth and empowerment of the other . . . neither submissive nor subordinate, nor superior, but aligned with the students in following their endeavours and achieving the goals of the school.
>
> (Brandes and Ginnis 1990: 30)

From the comments of many of the student groups interviewed it was clear that the heads themselves also engaged in such 'authentic' relationships with their students. Some of the secondary heads made a point of maintaining a high teaching profile, in order to keep contact and help build such relationships. One taught for seven out of a possible thirty periods in the school week. Students often recognized the symbolic nature of such a commitment:

> The fact that he teaches is important – he knows what pupils are like and what is going on in the school. He is good at communicating with the pupils, and they enjoy his lessons.
>
> (Secondary student)

However, most heads were able to achieve such relationships primarily through a high degree of social interaction on a daily basis with a large proportion of their students:

> She is always there at dinner times – getting to know the children and their names.
>
> (Primary student)

> He's there to welcome children when they arrive. He knows each child very well.
>
> (Parent of primary student)

The act of talking to students seemed to imply that the heads in our study had respect for them:

She talks to us as young adults.

(Year 6 student)

He's always got time to talk to you. On the second day I ever started in school he came up to me and said 'Hello Jessica.' I was gobsmacked.

(Secondary student)

He talks to you . . . I think [the head] is running a blinding school, and he's got blinding relationships with all the boys and that. The boys basically do what he says.

(Secondary student)

These heads not only made themselves available to talk to their students; it seems that they actively solicited their attention. They seemed to go to enormous lengths to facilitate such contact. One head took home the photographs of all new students in the summer holiday before their arrival, and memorized their names. The six student groups interviewed at his school all talked with affection about his daily lunchtime walk around the school grounds with the deputy head (who also memorized their names), and their friendly conversations with everyone they met.

They even talk to the yobs.

(Year 9 student)

You get to know him fairly quickly. I've never heard him shout.

(Year 9 student, same school)

His family is very important, and the school is his second family.

(Year 11 student, same school)

Other heads apparently took similar trouble:

He knows our names.

(Year 2 student)

I'm impressed when she knows my child's name when I meet her out shopping.

(Parent of primary student)

The personal knowledge of people and the concomitant ability to provide emotional support, recognized by teachers and support staff, were also acknowledged by students:

> The school trip was a nice break. She acted more like an auntie.
>
> (Year 6 student)

> She's always there for pupils 24 hours a day. I don't mean she's a saint, just a good human being.
>
> (Primary teacher)

> She always knows something about you, where you live, what team you support, who your friends are, and if you like school or not. She's sound in that way, like she cares about you.
>
> (Secondary student)

There was nothing contrived about these meetings, and the heads involved had worked hard at making them a normal part of the school day. They were clearly an important catalyst in the socialization and commitment to the values of the school of the students interviewed.

Students recognized the powerful support which such relationships could provide:

> The staff are not anxious when she comes into their classroom – she is not 'bossy', considers ideas and helps sort out lots of problems.
>
> (Primary student)

> There was less feeling in this school during Ofsted than in other schools.
>
> (Year 9 student)

> He pulled the school through the bereavement of a pupil.
>
> (Year 9 student)

They also recognized the difficulties that could arise when such relationships broke down, or were threatened by the head having to exercise discipline:

> She is nervous speaking to parents about problems.
>
> (Year 6 student)

Some heads clearly preferred to delegate the exercise of discipline, rather than compromise their general demeanour and endanger the relationships upon which they placed such value:

> Students see me as taking the school forward. I receive daily briefings on problem students, but I have others who do the heavy bit . . .
>
> (Secondary head)

The deputy tells more people off than her.

> (Year 6 student)

He doesn't like telling people off.

> (Primary student)

Students, in common with the other groups interviewed, recognized the interpersonal skills of their headteachers. Many of the qualities of the headteachers highlighted by students are echoed by other groups – good communication skills, enthusiasm, care and concern, availability and approachability. As with the other groups, this personal commitment of headteachers to building relationships had a powerful effect upon building commitment to the head's core values, and upon creating a sense of community which provided both emotional support and a sense of order for many of the students in the school.

Professional leadership

The concern shown by the headteachers in seeking the educational growth and empowerment of their students was overtly transmitted both in the literature produced by the school and, perhaps more importantly, in the daily communications and social intercourse between head, staff and students. This concern had a dual emphasis. The first was one for the welfare of all students:

> This school exudes caring, and all pupils are well looked after here.
>
> (Primary teacher)

> It's a tremendous help when you know it's always there for you and they'll do their best for you.
>
> (Primary student, same school)

If people come to this school, they fit in really quickly.
(Primary student)

The concern reported was indiscriminate:

She does not give up on anybody – she makes sure that children with special needs are provided with the assistance they need to help them learn.
(Primary student)

He even treats those not working hard as human beings.
(Year 11 student)

As well as an awareness that support was available when required, students also knew that there was a reciprocal need on their part to respond to the head's, and school's, expectations. The celebration of excellence was an important element in the public expression of such expectations. In one primary school the students cited the school's Ofsted report and its SATs results as evidence of the high standards the head had set. In a secondary school a formal but private ceremony was witnessed where the head personally handed out certificates and prizes for academic achievement and good attendance, but where students were not embarrassed by public exposure. National Records of Achievement were typed out for presentation to students when they left the school.

Other schools in the study also demonstrated this combination of expectation and celebration:

She rewards good work which makes you feel proud – even the teachers get 'good work' stickers to wear.
(Primary student)

He sets high standards of traditional excellence, and the school has achieved the excellence he has always desired, making the school popular with both pupils and parents.
(Secondary student)

It's a school where you have got to learn and where you have to buck up your ideas.
(Secondary student)

Students were also generally aware of the problems caused for heads by those who failed to respond to this culture of welfare and achievement:

She finds bullies frustrating – they're against the family
message of the school.

> (Year 6 student)

She doesn't let all the naughty people mess about . . .

> (Primary student)

The high expectations of behaviour and academic performance
expressed by heads had a profound effect upon many of the
students interviewed. There was a recognition that all students,
in exchange for the safe and caring environment to which the
head contributed, were expected to work hard, and that hard
work would be rewarded. We find here an acknowledgement of
the 'tough love' articulated overtly and practised by many of the
heads.

Values and vision

The heads had been instrumental in creating and maintaining a
vision for their schools, saw this as an important part of their job
and spent considerable time and effort in communicating this
vision to their students. Students in all the schools were therefore able to relate, in some detail, the core personal values held
by their respective headteachers which informed their educational practice and vision. In one secondary school, for example,
the moral leadership provided on a one-to-one basis to individual students translated easily to that provided to the whole
school on more formal occasions. We observed an assembly which
outlined the temptations offered in their everyday lives to Year
10 students, and the importance of establishing a work ethic in
preparation for the academic trials which lay ahead.

Heads were as explicit in their views in other schools. They
expected their students to value learning:

> [The head] wants children to do their best, be confident
> about going to secondary school, be happy about their work.
>
> (Primary student)

> He became a teacher because he wanted to teach, to help
> people learn, not only because he likes children . . .
>
> (Primary student)

and to show respect and concern for others:

> The head expects pupils to provide comfort for others if needed, be good-mannered at all times, do unto others as you would like to be treated yourself.
>
> (Primary student)

> He likes students . . . to be polite even out of school, to be smart and to observe the dress code. He does not like bullying and pupils chewing gum.
>
> (Secondary student)

The sense of equity and justice which some teachers valued in the featured heads is reflected in the comments of many students, of which this is typical:

> You know where you are with [her] – she tells you straight, no messing. She deals with everyone just the same, which is good. If you've done wrong then you get punished, but if you haven't she knows it and lets you off.
>
> (Secondary student)

The personal values of many of the heads derived from profoundly held religious beliefs. Students in most cases were aware of these beliefs, which clearly had been conveyed unassumedly by the heads concerned:

> She has Christian beliefs. She has a lot of belief in us as well.
>
> (Primary student)

> He has a faith, but he doesn't ram it down your throat.
>
> (Year 11 student)

> He's quite religious . . . his own background, the way he's been brought up.
>
> (Year 11 student)

Students also recognized the integrity in all that the heads did:

> He *never* shows that he is cross with the staff in front of the children.
>
> (Primary student)

> People can talk to her without being scared – she always keeps things confidential.
>
> (Primary student)

The head's provision of a role model, recognized by teachers and parents, was acknowledged by students:

> He and the staff set an example of courtesy and dress.
>
> (Secondary student)

> Students have a lot of respect for him as a person, not just as a head.
>
> (Year 13 student)

Heads clearly hoped that their core values would be assimilated by students as effectively as they had been by this one:

> You would feel ashamed if she told you off in class – it is an incentive to be well-behaved.
>
> (Primary student)

However, it was apparent that heads often had to combine their concern with a certain toughness:

> It is very difficult when children are naughty – he finds it hard to give out punishments because of his feelings for them. He finds time to listen to problems and he enjoys explaining things until you understand – he is prepared to go into detail to achieve this.
>
> (Primary student)

> When the nut tightens up it's definitely a hard school to get through. As you go up the school you get more privileges.
>
> (Secondary student)

> I'd say discipline – don't let them get away with anything . . . I reckon that is what [the head] is doing. Otherwise the school wouldn't run so good really.
>
> (Secondary student, same school)

Hard work was also an important element in the culture of the featured schools. There was a general awareness of the hard work undertaken by the heads, who consciously or otherwise provided modelling for students' behaviour:

> She is always busy.
>
> (Primary student)

> He works very hard, [as well as] always talking over the mistakes you have made, so that you won't make the same mistake again.
>
> (Primary student)

His own efforts are sometimes inspirational.

(Year 9 student)

The personal cost was sometimes recognized:

I don't think being a head is a good job. You have to work too hard. Some days [the head] looks knackered – sorry, very tired.

(Secondary student)

Students, in common with teachers, support staff, parents and governors, recognized the importance of the head as a role model. In common with these other groups, students identified their heads' core values of honesty, integrity, hard work, respect and concern for others. This concern manifested itself in a variety of ways, ranging from the tough treatment of behaviour which fell short of the standards demanded, to something perceived as close to love by some students.

Strategic leadership

Students recognized that their school had 'a way of doing things', and that the head was instrumental in building this strong culture. There was an achievement culture in all the featured schools:

She wants pupils to do their best and to get good SATs results.

(Primary student)

She wants pupils to do well – the teachers have the same attitude. Do well *always*.

(Primary student)

He sets high standards of traditional excellence – good examination results, good school teams, good drama productions and good music teaching.

(Secondary student)

Students recognized that difficulties arose where heads were unable, for reasons sometimes beyond their control, to sustain a school's culture:

He has tried his best to get things sorted out, but this has not always been possible . . . It is sometimes difficult to recruit and retain staff, and this can cause difficult classroom situations and disaffected children.

(Secondary student)

This recognition was most marked in the schools where the head was a comparative newcomer, and where memories of the last head contributed to the collective consciousness:

She didn't realize what the school was like at first, but she knows it better now. She's talked to us more.

(Year 6 student)

This particular head introduced bells to mark the beginning and end of lessons, as well as a dress code for staff. Yet beyond these symbolic gestures, the comments of staff as well as students in the school suggested that any change would need to be incremental, and almost blended into the culture which she had inherited from an extremely popular predecessor. Her students recognized their own part in generating shared beliefs:

She relies on us to set an example.

(Year 6 student, same school)

In a school with a longer established head, this function of progressing the culture of the school had been completely absorbed into the consciousness of some students, so that certain kinds of behaviour had become reflexes:

I would feel guilty about misbehaviour, because of my respect for him.

(Year 11 student)

Student behaviour here had been directly influenced by the ability of the head to proselytize his set of core values.

Students were again as perceptive as teachers, governors and parents of the head's role in establishing the culture of their school, and quite young students showed how aware they were of the tensions which arose when a new head attempted to change that culture.

Metaphors

The metaphors of headship offered by the students interviewed reflected the various facets of the job they perceived the head as doing. There was a strong sense of the direction which the head gave to the school: he was 'leader of the world', 'driver of the train' and 'leader of the pack' to the students in one primary school; in another:

> a ship's captain, because she takes on a lot of responsibility and she heads us in the right direction . . .
>
> (Primary student)

and a 'captain or coach, but not a referee' in a third. A secondary student saw the head as 'the director of a business – powerful and in control'.

Some of the images of direction suggested a slightly more passive, covert approach. One primary head was seen as 'the queen bee', at the centre of her hive. A secondary head was seen by one student as

> the biggest branch of a corporate tree, pointing energetically outwards and upwards . . .

and by another as

> a polka-dot plant, ever widening its territorial roots but not harming other neighbouring plants in the process.

The image of the head as an energy source was a recurring theme. One head was seen as

> the sun at the centre of the solar system – providing light and warmth *and* controlling the movement of the planets.
>
> (Primary student)

Another primary head was seen as

> the clockwork inside a clock – making everything go . . .

> a computer system controller . . .

and

> an engine in the car, with lots of energy to get things moving.

In the same spirit a secondary head was seen by one of his male students as

> a rugby scrum-half, organizing the scrum and the three-quarters, feeding in the ball and passing it on, though rarely running with it.

One of his female students, using a parallel image, saw him as

> a netball centre, pivotal to the team but never scoring.

Some of the images recognized the emphasis placed by the heads upon student welfare. Two primary heads were compared to 'a shepherd, caring for every member of the flock'. The image was reinforced in one school with the suggestion that the previous head would have lost the odd sheep. One of the two heads was also

> a gardener, who plants flowers and shrubs, and tends them as they grow.

Secondary students also provided some powerful welfare images: one head was seen as

> the babysitter – he looks after everybody . . .

> a sergeant – respectable, reliable, thoughtful and caring . . .

and

> like a dad – he never gives up on you, is someone to look up to, has courage and authority (but is not authoritarian).

Another was seen as

> a godfather, a grandfather, giving advice without exercising discipline . . .

> a priest, leading by personal example rather than coercion . . .

and

> Father Christmas all year round.

Aspects of the problem-solving role of headteachers were acknowledged especially by primary students, and in particular those relating to the regulation of student behaviour:

> He's a detective, always on the case, sniffing out trouble and finding the evidence.
>
> (Primary student)

> She's like a detective, because she always wants to get to the bottom of it.
>
> (Primary student)

A policewoman on the beat.

> (Primary student)

A judge in court keeping everything in order.

> (Primary student, same school)

An owl.

> (Primary student)

The same students were aware of the tension between the welfare and disciplinary roles of their headteachers, and a number of their suggested images reflected this tension. One primary head was likened to

an armadillo – crunchy on the outside and soft on the inside.

A Year 6 student in another school commented that the head

has a thorny side, but her petals are soft.

The same head was seen by another of her students as

a mother lioness or tiger, fighting the corner of her cubs.

This particular head also spawned a series of images which suggested that the students perceived the reconciliation of these roles as a purposeful but often lonely job – she was variously described as 'a beaver', 'a mountain goat striving forever upwards', and 'a swan'.

As a group the students responded more spontaneously than the adult members of the school community when asked to identify metaphors of headship. There are a number of possible explanations. The students interviewed may have been selected by heads because they were articulate, and they also appeared to be less inhibited than the adults interviewed. Students, particularly in primary schools, showed less awareness in their responses of certain aspects of the head's role, for example their part in curriculum development, planning, monitoring and budget management, and were therefore presenting images relating to a less complex notion of what headship entailed than that held, for example, by teachers. Teachers in particular found it difficult to embrace what they saw as a complex job into a single image. But finally, the power of many of the images presented by students bore testimony to the close personal relationship which many of them felt that they had with their headteachers. In the same way that the heads felt that they knew their students as individuals, students' images of their headteachers suggested that the feeling was reciprocated. The images showed an insight into headship from students who were on intimate terms with their headteachers.

Conclusion

Students observed their headteachers performing in a greater variety of settings within their schools than any of the other groups interviewed in this study. There was an awareness that headteachers took part in the administration of the school, but much of this was invisible to students. Consequently, their views of their headteachers were based almost entirely upon the perceptions derived from their observations and personal contact.

The heads were recognized as having good interpersonal skills, and as holding a set of core values centred around student achievement and welfare. They were seen as role models in the daily application of these core values. The warmth and richness of many of the students' responses reflected the esteem felt for the various headteachers. Students recognized the important contribution of the head's core values to the smooth running of the school and to the integrity of the school community.

7

SCHOOL LEADERSHIP: TENSIONS AND DILEMMAS

. . . whether we like it or not, under new public sector management, there are emerging irreconcilable goals for schooling. On the one hand there are those who are pushing schools to operate like businesses, and to pursue the educational equivalent of profit maximisation. On the other hand, schools are ultimately concerned with the development of students who are not only employable, but also autonomous, responsible, moral individuals who are effective members of society . . . Heads who are able to model moral leadership in the way they run their schools are more likely, in our view, to concentrate on the ultimate goal of schooling, even though they are constantly under pressure to do otherwise . . .

(Dempster and Mahoney 1998: 137–8)

This chapter explores the parameters of leadership as experienced by headteachers in the study. In particular, it considers the tensions and dilemmas faced by these and other headteachers in the current educational climate. The stakeholders' responses revealed a complex picture of leadership which, although related to existing models of leadership, did not wholly endorse or confirm their main theoretical perspectives. The analysis revealed that they viewed the headteachers as exhibiting similar sets of 'leadership characteristics' and managing broadly similar sets of tensions and dilemmas. Although the heads were at different stages in their careers, of different ages, had different experiences and were working in very different contexts (see Table 2.1) there was a core set of characteristics recognized from all the chosen perspectives. The chapter focuses on some of these tensions and dilemmas in order to convey a sense of the relationship between the characterization of effective headteachers, the tensions that surrounded them and the leadership dilemmas which they faced.

As the previous chapters have revealed, the various stakeholders shared a broadly similar construction of 'leadership'. The fact that a shared construction existed across such a variety of groups and disparate contexts is perhaps unsurprising when one considers the emphasis placed in the media, literature, folklore, as well as in the profession itself, on what constitutes a 'good' leader. For example, the various stakeholders tended to agree on the need for 'bravery', 'openness', 'honesty', 'good decision making', 'people skills' and 'vision'. However, in relation to existing leadership theories there were a number of common characteristics that emerged which were somewhat different from those identified in previous studies of effective leadership (e.g. Sammons *et al.* 1997).

The presence of a shared social construction of effective leadership among very different stakeholders is significant for three reasons. First, it helped us realize the extent to which we were gleaning from the various stakeholders not just observed characteristics of their headteachers, but also beliefs about how 'good' leaders should act. Such beliefs have their roots within shared social constructions of what leadership is about and the way in which leaders should act. These formed a complex matrix of demands and expectations around the headteachers which they partially assimilated, always had to manage and occasionally challenged. Second, the analysis had begun to reveal patterns within the expectations of different groups of stakeholders who gave greater significance to certain characteristics because of their position within the school and its broader community. For example, honesty and openness in decision making was seen as particularly significant by teachers whose careers and working conditions were directly affected by them; parents placed particular value on their headteacher's ability to communicate and draw them into the community of the school; and governors emphasized the strategic and micro-political skills of headteachers. Each headteacher's work was, therefore, set within a matrix of needs and expectations all of which had to be navigated. Third, this 360 degree matrix of expectations and demands placed on the headteachers by the broader school community formed the backdrop to a number of tensions and dilemmas. Not only did it play a part in their construction, but it also represented a number of critical audiences as the headteachers attempted to lead and manage them.

Tensions and dilemmas

Damned if you do and damned if you don't. That seems to be the message.

(Ball 1987: 164)

In this chapter use is made of two linked concepts – tensions and dilemmas – which are grounded in the data as 'lenses' (Berlak and Berlak 1981) through which to focus in on leadership. The main distinction between tensions and dilemmas concerns the possibilities of choice and influence. The tensions identified in this study tended to be those over which headteachers had little choice or influence. In the case of the dilemmas, possibilities of choice and influence did exist, but the degree to which the heads exercised such possibilities varied considerably. A dilemma, in this sense, is a situation which presents at least two contradictory propositions. Whichever is chosen, however, will not be entirely satisfactory. Together these constructs of 'tensions' and 'dilemmas' capture the immediacy of the continuing conflicts faced by many of the heads in the study. They underscore the continuing dynamic between their core personal values, management functions and leadership demands. They capture their past, present and future pressures, challenges, and the concerns and aspirations with which they are faced daily and which reflect the multifaceted demands of the role. Heads are constantly juggling competing demands upon their time, energy and resources.

The data revealed seven key tensions and three dilemmas of 'effective' headteachers which focus upon their roles not only in maintaining and consolidating what they have already achieved, but also in managing the challenges associated with moving their individual schools forward. The tensions focus broadly on issues of leadership and management; personal time and professional tasks; personal and institutional values; development and maintenance; internal and external change; autocracy and autonomy; and leadership in small schools. They reflect the concerns of a group of headteachers who are primarily concerned with achieving success for the teachers and pupils in their schools, for whom improvement is a permanent part of their personal and professional agendas.

Seven tensions of school leadership

Leadership versus management

Increased responsibilities of the headteacher in the twenty-first century to manage diverse aspects of school organization may be construed as redefining the headteacher as 'managing director'. Yet, at the same time the impetus for improvement in schools via externally initiated change has placed a greater emphasis upon the leadership role of the head. While it is evident that management and leadership as constructs overlap, they remain qualitatively different functions. Leadership is essentially the process of building and maintaining a sense of vision for the organization whereas, in contrast, management is the co-ordination, support and monitoring of organizational activities. To maintain the organization, i.e. to run the school, requires management action, but to develop and transform the school requires personal and professional qualities and values to which all involved in the school community can willingly subscribe. To enact both roles fully necessitates a careful balancing act. Thus, one common tension facing heads is how to be both a manager and a leader.

The heads and others in this study were able to distinguish between 'leadership' and 'management' activities. One head commented, for example, that 'management was concerned with running the ship' while leadership was concerned with 'setting the course'. They were also able to distinguish different interpretations of leadership.

Deputy heads commented:

You have to have a vision for the school and the practical know-how of how to get it there. The head has the inter-personal, practical and technical skills to do this. She can walk on water, or so it seems! . . . Leadership and management overlap, but prime responsibility for leadership rests with the head – when she is absent an experienced deputy can do the management. Leadership involves inspiring others, as well as developing and supporting them – that requires skill and confidence.

(Secondary deputy)

Leadership is about having vision and articulating, ordering priorities, getting others to go with you, constantly review-ing what you are doing and holding on to things you value. Management is about the functions, procedures and sys-tems by which you realize the vision.

(Primary deputy)

However, despite being able to delineate between leadership and management, there was still an acknowledgement that there might be differential performance in carrying out leadership and management functions. For example, one deputy head com-mented about her headteacher:

She's a good leader but she's a better manager, because she's doing things yesterday. She will have fifteen things going on at the same time and she will have her finger on every single one of them. I couldn't do that. I am a bit more methodical.

(Infant deputy)

A contributory factor to the 'leadership versus management' tension concerns the interpretation of headship. If headship is construed as being mainly about administration and organiza-tion, then being a head is simply being a manager. Alternatively, if, as the literature suggests, leadership is a paramount feature of successful schools, then headship should be more than just management. The tension facing most heads in this study was how to combine effective leadership and management strategies so that they reinforced each other. The tensions between leadership and management which were identified tended to be associated with time and priorities. The 'time to manage' was seen by a number of heads as the major difficulty facing them.

> I'd like to be a better leader but I know that if there's a crisis I have to manage that straight away. I'd like to lead more but where do I get the time?
>
> (Infant head)

They acknowledged that they faced increasing demands upon their time and as a result were tempted to deal with those issues, or problems, that were the most immediate and pressing. Though they managed priorities so that they were not dictated by the events of the day, heads felt that they spent too much of their time being reactive rather than proactive. A continuing tension they faced, then, was one of finding time both to develop the school and to maintain it.

Although the majority of heads in this study had been successful in this endeavour, there was wide acknowledgement that this had not been achieved without cost. Achieving a balance between the two roles was far from straightforward and often required significant personal and professional sacrifice. The result was a values-led, principled contingency form of leadership which was neither wholly transactional nor wholly transformational, though heads did achieve change.

Development versus maintenance

The daily world of the school is primarily concerned with transacting information and maintaining the organization, rather than with transforming through developing others. A further challenge identified in the study arising from the leadership–management tension concerned the extent to which they were responsible for development as opposed to maintenance of their school. For example, the majority of heads recognized that the teachers were the greatest asset in ensuring high-quality learning opportunities for pupils and that further developing their teaching skills and abilities was crucial to improved performance. However, there was also an acknowledgement of the political and social imperatives imposed upon schools that demanded compliance and conformity. Hence, for headteachers who want to develop and transform the practice of others, the demands of the system often create a tension:

> How do you reconcile the management of paper with the management of people? I spend too much time in my office with bits of paper and precious little time with the people that count.
>
> (Infant head)

This tension had been addressed by many heads in the study through a process of delegation and reprioritization. Many of the heads had ensured that they allowed time for the development of others in the school by allocating more routine tasks and responsibilities to others:

> I have an excellent deputy head who looks after certain aspects of school management for me. This enables me to focus on what really matters, the staff and the pupils.
>
> (Infant head)

> If I don't develop others, the school won't develop. So that's my priority; other jobs can be delegated but not this one.
>
> (Primary head)

Like other tensions felt by the heads in the study, the tension of transaction versus transformation was not easily resolved. For many heads, 'top-down' demands dictated the way they worked. For example:

> I'd like to develop the school but I'm swamped by demands from outside that have to be done yesterday.
>
> (Infant head)

Other heads managed this tension by putting staff needs first as far as they possibly could.

> My staff come first at all times but you cannot ignore outside pressures. You need to be selective about the way you respond and not forget the teaching staff and their needs.
>
> (Infant head)

It was recognized that this particular tension was likely to increase as more demands and new policy initiatives are produced. However, the majority of heads in the study remain committed to their staff and their development, seeing this as central to the ongoing improvement of their school.

Internal versus external change

The growth in the external scrutiny and monitoring of schools has created its own sets of tensions. Headteachers now find themselves positioned uneasily between those outside schools instigating and promoting changes and their own staff within school who will ultimately have to implement them. Even when not caught directly between these groups headteachers can find themselves trying to offer leadership in a context where their teachers' performance is being set against that of colleagues in other departments or even nearby schools.

> A headteacher now has much less autonomy and is account-able to so many people – staff, parents, governors, LEA – he has to manage externally driven change.
>
> (Secondary head)

> We are in a culture of managing change and accountability. The pressure is from outside but I have to manage the pres-sure inside. There are external and internal drivers for change!!
>
> (Secondary head)

These 'internal drivers' for change can be characterized as a complex mixture of school-based factors, i.e. the institutional needs and wants which provide the impetus for the school's development. Some of these internal drivers are 'givens' in that they would exist irrespective of the type of leadership approach adopted. Other internal drivers are 'constructed' by leaders within the school by their commitment to a particular vision, values framework or strategies of management. The 'external drivers' arise from policy interventions and edicts that require com-pliance. Increasingly headteachers, and those around them, are aware of being caught between these two sets of drivers. The pressure of external initiatives on the leadership of the head-teacher is summarized in the following observation made by a deputy headteacher:

> Changes are externally imposed so that the head must inter-pret incoming documents before she can inform the staff. The speed with which those changes have had to be intro-duced means that she has had little time to motivate staff and she is finding it increasingly difficult to justify imposing

yet more demands for change. It also makes it more difficult
to see things through – she has had to learn to delegate
more of the responsibility for managing change.

(Infant deputy)

The impact that responding to external changes has had on a
headteacher's ability to lead is illustrated in the above quote.
Staff morale can be affected by 'yet more demands for change',
energies can become dissipated and professional lives fragmented
by too many changes which often mean that pressing internal
issues are not attended to.

Externally imposed changes also challenge headteachers' sense
that as leaders they have the ability to shape the school in line
with their vision and their style of working. Headteachers who
are used to being proactive rather than reactive have had to
learn how to deal with a more or less constant flow of initiatives. They now have to demonstrate their leadership by the
selection of which initiatives they take on; the relative support
which they provide for their implementation; their knowledge
of how others are tackling new initiatives; and how well they
can adapt initiatives that are forced on them to their particular
circumstances.

Autocracy versus autonomy

The changing face of leadership has meant that decision making
within an organization is no longer the exclusive preserve of the
headteacher. Indeed, leadership theory has advocated a move
from transactional forms of leadership to more transformational
modes where decision making is shared and devolved. The practical reality of this situation means that heads have to decide
how far the boundaries of autocracy and democracy coincide.
On the one hand they have ultimate authority to make decisions because of their positional and referential power. On the
other hand, the research evidence concerning successful schools
indicates that a collaborative leadership style reaps huge benefits
for the organization.

The study revealed that a degree of autonomy concerning
decision making tended to be equated with effective leadership
but that heads were seen as having the right to take the ultimate
decisions at critical times:

Although we can work closely there has to be a time when decisions are taken and she has to say whether we can or cannot do this . . . There has to be an ultimate authority where she sees the overall pattern.

(Primary deputy)

He can be quite ruthless when he wants to be. But you can see where his decision is coming from.

(Primary deputy)

While there was a good deal of day-to-day autonomy, the authority of the headteacher was final. The tension between autocracy and consultation varied among heads in the study. It may be that collaborative decision-making processes can only be achieved once heads have established themselves as leaders within the school:

Once you've established yourself you can be a little more of a democratic leader and . . . give people their head . . . When you are struggling in the early days of getting an organization sorted out you can't afford too many mistakes . . .

(Special school head)

Once again, this tension is not easily resolved and is highly dependent upon the values and leadership style of the head-teacher. However, the study did demonstrate that the heads varied in their leadership strategies and were able to judge when to be autocratic rather than consultative and which situations required each approach.

Personal time versus professional tasks

The increasing external requirements upon schools have led many headteachers to take more and more of their personal time for professional purposes. The need to complete an increasing number of tasks has forced heads to reallocate their personal time and to spend a greater proportion of their time at school or out of school on school-related business. Most of the heads in the study recognized this tension and acknowledged that the demands of the job were, at times, excessive:

> I work at least 60 hours a week. I find I am much more tired now in the evenings but I do work long hours here ... it worries me because I don't know how long I can go on putting in the amount of energy.
>
> (Primary head)

> There is too much paperwork ... I have a sense of failing constantly because tasks take much longer and there is not enough time to do everything.
>
> (Infant head)

All the headteachers worked long hours and played a variety of complex roles within their schools, and they all talked of the ways in which they managed to survive such pressures. For some, staying physically fit was a priority through a variety of sporting activities. For others, the support networks of family and friends were vital in taking them away from the everyday pressures of school:

> I manage to keep sane by visiting the local gym and keeping myself fit.
>
> (Primary head)

> I am lucky to have a supportive, loving family and the support of my Church to see me through the stressful times.
>
> (Primary head)

> We have good friends ... none of them in education ... who are a godsend. We do things together regularly ... which helps maintain my sanity.
>
> (Secondary head)

For all the headteachers in the study the pressure upon time was a common and consistent problem. Despite their various means of managing stress, the personal time and energy of most heads was eroded by the demands of the job. In several cases this had had a detrimental effect upon their home lives and had sometimes resulted in personal sacrifice:

> The stress of the job meant that I was working long hours

and not seeing my family. They finally had enough and I had to recognize that the job was destroying my home life.

(Primary head)

At the end of the day, it's just a job and other things are more important, like having a personal life.

(Secondary head)

Although most headteachers in the study had found ways of managing the stress and demands of the job and all recognized the importance of carefully balancing home and work, for some the personal opportunity costs were still proving unacceptably high and potentially damaging to their personal lives in the longer term.

Personal values versus institutional imperatives

At the end of the day the head has to have integrity and . . . to stick to core values and beliefs. It is important that the head can demonstrate integrity in the face of adversity and can show a moral purpose against all odds . . .

(Primary head)

A principled headteacher may believe that those who work in the school should have space to develop and work with their own educational values. But as a manager the head is also committed to setting and embedding institutional values. The tension here arises because of the way in which different sets of values might be mediated. The issue is whether there is room for different sets of values within one educational organization. If the values of the school are clearly shared and articulated then the possible tensions around values may not exist. However, if they are not shared, or if they are imposed from outside, values may be contested and tensions may arise.

The study revealed that all the headteachers held strong sets of personal values that shaped and influenced the value base of the school. In most cases, these values were shared by staff, governors and parents, or at least respected because of their positive influence upon the school:

He holds traditional human values – care for people and community and giving back to society the benefits of what

you have been given at school. You are a better person if
you achieve academically, but that is only part of being a
whole balanced person. He is politically driven and his personal attitudes are underpinned by his spiritual beliefs.

(Primary teacher)

She believes in: accountability for the pupils' achieving their
full potential; that schools should provide a caring and supportive environment in which children can be happy at
whatever they are doing; having high expectations of the
pupils; professional autonomy of teachers coupled with
accountability for their actions.

(Primary teacher)

He provides child-centred leadership – the pupils' social
and educational development, security and well-being are
paramount.

(Primary teacher, different school)

While I might not agree wholeheartedly with her Christian
beliefs, I can see that her love of children and her desire to
see them do well is the driving force behind the school.

(Infant teacher)

While there was little evidence in the study of opposing sets of
values within the schools, tensions did arise when outside values
were imposed upon schools. For example, the externally driven
value base imposed currently upon schools is one of accountability, effectiveness and efficiency. Operating within the value
system of the 'quasi-market' place clearly raised some tensions
for heads:

I find that I cannot reconcile myself to the language of business. It has no place in school and no relevance to education.

(Infant head)

I find myself torn between wanting to be a managing director and an educator. I don't think you can be both and
therefore, I feel I am always compromising my personal
values.

(Secondary head)

The heads in the study had clear and strongly held values that
positively influenced the school. In almost all cases staff and

others in the community shared this value base and exemplified this in their interactions with other staff and pupils. The tension with competing values from outside the school for many heads was irreconcilable. One head saw it as an 'inevitable tension' of being externally and internally accountable. Yet, part of the reason for the effectiveness of heads in the study was that while recognizing this tension they did not sacrifice their sets of personal values on the altar of political expediency.

Leadership in small versus large schools

The study showed that there was a leadership tension directly related to the size of the school. This tension was particularly acute for small schools in the study which felt disadvantaged on two main counts. The first concerned the small number of staff and the diverse subject needs of the national curriculum. One small school within the study had only 90+ pupils and two full-time and three part-time staff. The head acknowledged that this created a tension around curriculum coverage and subject specialism:

> In terms of how we manage the curriculum I suppose we do it slightly differently from a large school. There isn't the same scope for flexibility. I am not a scientist at all and I found that I was spending long hours preparing science. There is an issue here about curriculum coverage that is not apparent in secondary schools.
>
> (Primary head)

A second concern was the full-time teaching responsibilities of the headteacher. The fact that heads in small schools tend to have a significant classroom teaching commitment results in tensions between teaching, leadership and management which create unique sets of development issues. The 'teaching head' may be a phenomenon in large schools also but the time spent on teaching by such heads is usually minimal. The teaching load of heads in very small primary schools leaves little time for managing, or leading the school:

> I would like to be able to try and do the job without the constraints of being a class teacher as well. If we could afford for me not to be a class teacher, if I had enough

people just for me to be teaching some of the time that would be fine. But I think it's all the stress of planning and preparing and co-ordinating as a class teacher which is too much . . . I actually feel that in a small school headship is actually not a very good career move. There are deputies in larger schools who actually teach less than me. They've got the time to develop leadership skills

(Primary head)

It is evident that the types of leadership demands upon the heads of small primary schools are different from those upon heads of large primary and secondary schools. The scale of the school as an organization inevitably places differential pressure upon heads throughout the system. Issues of leadership and management are different in a school where there are less than 100 pupils. This creates additional tensions to those already out-lined in this chapter which are not sector- or size-specific but represent generic tensions faced by headteachers throughout the UK and possibly further afield.

Three dilemmas

The headteachers, and those around them, recognized that a key part of being a leader was being able to deal with tensions, and that their effectiveness was in part defined by their ability and willingness to cope with the 'tough' decision and the dilemma it may represent. Dilemmas whose origins lie outside the school add to those created from within which may relate to different views of 'effective' leadership approaches, student–teacher rela-tionships and teaching standards. A further point of origin of certain dilemmas was the personal philosophies and value frame-works of the headteachers themselves, i.e. the strong moral basis of much of their leadership discussed in the previous chapters. In the following section three leadership dilemmas are discussed.

Development versus dismissal

The first dilemma is one with which most headteachers have to deal in their careers. It can be summed up in the following question: 'What do I do with a member of staff whose poor teaching is having an adverse effect on the education of the pupils and whose performance doesn't seem to be improving no matter what I do in terms of support and staff development?' For people who have to 'make tough decisions' this particular problem creates a leadership dilemma because the continuing failure of an individual member of staff cuts across their personal framework of values and beliefs:

> I have a core belief in equal opportunities for all and I try to let this determine my leadership style.
>
> (Secondary head)

The headteachers' deeply held belief in the potential of all, and the possibility of developing everyone within the community of their school, lay at the heart of their philosophies of leadership:

> I live by my Christian beliefs and I try to run this school by Christian values.
>
> (Infant head)

> The well-being of the staff and the children is the most important thing.
>
> (Primary head)

> When a child is here there should be no closed doors in their world.
>
> (Primary head)

However, if a member of staff began to represent one of those 'closed doors' then the headteacher was under a moral imperative to act:

> I think that is one of the things which is perhaps more difficult about management, as opposed to leadership, in teaching. If you are manager or a director of ICI and a member of staff has been giving problems there comes a point where you say, 'Oh I think this is it. I don't think it is in the interest of the organization that you continue.' In teaching it doesn't work like that. I find it really really hard that there is a class of children who nobody is pitching in for. You can support somebody who is incompetent for as long as you like but there comes a point where you know

that it is not going to make any difference, particularly if they have been doing it for a long time.

(Infant head)

The decision, however, still clashed with their ideological and educative commitment to the development of everyone in the school community. The 'failure' of a colleague was perceived as an admission of their own failure in key roles which were at the heart of their leadership – promoting staff development, remotivating staff, and changing the culture of a school:

> He respects people who can do the job that they set out to do . . . He's very much a people person . . . Not very good with paperwork. He has a lot of contact with staff and with parents . . . The vision is brilliant and the ideas and the initiatives.

(Primary teacher)

The potential negative impacts of the processes of dismissing a member of staff in the relatively small community of a school were widely recognized and added considerably to the tensions surrounding any decision. Thus, dealing with the impact of a dismissal on staff morale and sense of security was an important technical aspect of this particular dilemma.

A further associated aspect of the dilemma arose from the emphasis placed by so many of the heads on the quality of their relationships with staff. In Chapter 3 it was shown that the headteachers stressed the need to build supportive, and critical, relationships with staff:

> Leadership is the personal qualities that you bring to the relationships that you are dealing with.

(Secondary head)

> It's important that we are able to support one another personally as well as professionally . . . If they have an emergency or crisis at home, I'm going to respond to that . . . so that they feel valued as a person as well as a teacher.

(Primary head)

> As the years have worn by he has become more of a friend. He's really concerned with your personal life as well, how it affects you.

(Primary teacher)

These relationships were seen as a means of developing their leadership and establishing collaborative cultures, because it was through them that they communicated their views, consulted with staff and built up their influence on staff as a whole. The headteachers' relationships with their staff were also examples of their leadership in practice, as they enabled them to demonstrate care, support and knowledge alongside high expectations and challenge. A central element of their effectiveness as leaders in their communities was the quality of these relationships:

> They're my people that I pastorally look after . . . There is that sort of rapport . . . very rarely do I have to throw my weight around.
>
> (Primary head)

> It's to do with supporting staff and people feel that I support them. It's to do with motivating and appreciating staff's efforts . . . being interested in what they're doing and giving them feedback on a daily basis.
>
> (Infant head)

The dismissal of a member of staff by a headteacher, even when supported by other staff, touches upon the nature of the relationship between leaders and those they lead. It demonstrates to staff that their welfare is not the final arbiter in how their relationship with the headteacher will develop:

> If unpleasant things have to be done I don't shrink from it because I realize that I am likely to be improving things for the good of the children.
>
> (Primary head)

The dismissal of a member of staff highlights a clear boundary between the personal and professional relationships which are at the basis of the school community.

Power with or power over?

The second dilemma is based around the tensions created in developing a clear vision for a school based upon existing sets of core values held by the headteacher and building a cohesive staff team actively involved in its development, not all of whom may share those values. The basis of this dilemma is the extent to which both similar and dissimilar values can be reconciled.

The leadership challenge for the headteacher is to maintain an appropriate balance between establishing an agreed way forward and maintaining staff commitment and involvement. It is a question of whether heads exercise power 'over' or power 'with' their colleagues in developing the school:

> To have [teachers] on line and to agree, not to agree to everything but to understand the main aims and ambitions . . . Bringing them along with the challenge of what the LEA and government wants . . . To know how to get the best out of them . . . Getting that balance is the biggest challenge . . . Being able to pick out what's important and being able to manage staff . . .
>
> (Primary head)

For many of the headteachers in this research there was no direct contradiction between developing a cohesive staff and involving them in the running of the school:

> I aim to achieve cohesiveness amongst the staff. I hope that the staff have a direction and opportunities to do what they want to do and feel secure and confident in that. I always try to respect the individual . . . hopefully if I am respectful of their views and opinions I will make them feel valued.
>
> (Primary head)

Building a cohesive staff team was something that most of the headteachers had achieved over a considerable amount of time by careful recruitment and use of staff development time. However, the issues they faced then in terms of building a cohesive staff were related to their time in post and the opportunities they had had to recruit like-minded staff. For newer headteachers the willingness of their colleagues to 'buy into' their view of how the school should develop was a key concern:

> I dread when we've got to replace a teacher. It takes a long time to break a teacher in. I just look for personality really. I don't care if they've got a degree. I like people who can do a job but also do a job my way. I don't want them to be a clone but we don't want any of this loose cannon stuff.
>
> (Infant head)

In establishing a clear vision the headteachers all tended to use personalized criteria such as providing learning experiences of a quality which they would want their own children to experience (and with which colleagues would find it hard to disagree):

> What is achieved must be good enough for my own children; treat others as you would wish yourself to be treated.
>
> (Primary head)

> All pupils should grow into autonomous adults, able to achieve independence and excellence.
>
> (Secondary head)

> A belief, for the children, of high expectations no matter where they are coming from.
>
> (Infant head)

They also drew parallels between their aims for pupils and those for staff:

> Everybody is important, everybody has value and we stand for being able to allow every person in the school to achieve.
>
> (Primary head)

Through these kinds of statements heads established an inclusive philosophy for the treatment of everybody in the school community. In terms of achieving 'inclusivity' they sought to achieve a balance between consulting and involving the staff in their decisions and still providing a clear direction forward, another valued aspect of their leadership.

The natural extension to involving staff in the decisions about the school is the delegation of responsibility for their implementation. All the headteachers in these case studies were perceived as being effective at delegation, a crucial aspect of their technical and practical leadership:

> I have had responsibility to develop things I'm really interested in . . . and this is part of the head's leadership . . . I do a lot of spade work but [the head] has always come in and given me a chance to take it where I want to take it.
>
> (Primary deputy)

As the boundaries expand of the area which teachers control, they might well begin to argue that their unique understanding of that area makes them aware of the limited nature of the headteacher's view of the issues for which they are responsible.

Below two teachers reflect on their desire for more responsibility and involvement in the shaping of their schools:

> We are leaders in our own little domain and sometimes it's hard to accept the overall leadership . . . because you think you have got a better way of doing it.
>
> (Primary teacher)

> Perhaps [the headteacher] needs to take on now that he has very high calibre staff and this can actually be quite a boring job when we've got it all running so well. For some staff they are happy with that, for me I need more challenges I am afraid . . . I'm perhaps at the point now where I want to do something extra. He's got to try more, and maybe there are other staff as well who find it a little bit boring sitting in a classroom each and every day doing the same. We've reached that now . . . How do you deal with that one? That's difficult.
>
> (Special school teacher)

Some of the headteachers in the study deliberately managed the aspirations of their teachers to get more involved in the running of the school by using professional development opportunities as a way of keeping staff 'on board' as well as 'cooling them out':

> You've always got to give J [a teacher] a bone to play with otherwise he turns his ability, and he has a lot of ability, into the organization and becomes destructive . . . He's a six month man. He's a performer, he doesn't have to get into second gear to do well, but one of the characteristics of those people is that they don't stick at things. You've got to look for little angles to keep people on board, interested, because these aren't ordinary people.
>
> (Special school head)

The challenge of being a leader among other leaders is the political aspect of this particular dilemma. If the headteacher gets it right then the metaphors used about headteachers as 'spiders at the centre of a web' hint not just at the difficulty of integrating different perspectives within a school but also compliment them on their ability in doing this:

> Easy going and will allow other people to do things . . . doesn't save it all for himself . . . is not looking for all the

accolades. He doesn't want everything to be his idea, which
some people have a problem with. He's not bothered where
the ideas come from . . . We need space to develop our ideas
but of course we're not all going off at a tangent. The job of
the head is to know what is going on in each bit. Not so
much actually being the leader of the project . . . The head
is a co-ordinator as well as co-ordinating outside. A big
spider in the middle of the web, and he runs out here and
there.

> (Special school teacher)

The crux of the dilemma for some headteachers is when
'empowered' or 'liberated' staff decide that they 'may want to
take it' in a direction with which the headteacher disagrees. At
this point, however, headteachers may reserve their right to
take the final decision:

If we come to an impasse I will go over [and say], 'You've
got to do it, all right. You've had your debate. I've seen the
pros and cons [and] this is what is going to be done.' Then
I'll walk away and they'll accept.

> (Special school head)

It's his decision at the end of the day. He's always likely to
push the school further . . . taking new initiatives. He con-
sults us, asks us what we think but it will be his decision at
the end of the day . . . He makes it a challenge and we all
tend to rise to it . . . a good delegator.

> (Primary teacher)

Because there is a certain amount of negotiation and team
spirit people actually forget their role perhaps in the organization and perhaps think what they want ought to be the
overriding consideration. Because of this feeling that I have
that everybody is equal, that they all play an equally important role, pieces of jigsaw, sometimes it can cause friction
with other members of staff who think, 'Well I wanted this
and it's not happening', forgetting that you've got to see a
total picture.

> (Infant head)

If the headteacher gets it wrong, however, then rather more
unflattering political comparisons come to the fore:

> There is a dictatorial 'Machiavellian' side to the head which differs from his self-image as a 'benevolent dictator'.
>
> (Primary teacher)

The high level of personal commitment headteachers have to their school and staff and the costs this has for them make it difficult for them to accept the 'rejection' implicit within any staff member's decision to go in a different direction:

> He gets depressed if those behind him don't support him or misinterpret his actions or motives. That hurts him.
>
> (Secondary teacher)

As headteachers increasingly demonstrate their leadership through their relationships with staff then at any point of conflict the personal and organizational politics of their leadership may become conflated. This can carry with it its own dangers as the headteachers' actions cut across the notion of the school and staff as a 'family' and begin to reveal the power relationships which lie behind such a comforting image.

Subcontracting versus mediation?

> It is difficult to plan too far ahead because 'politics' may dictate further changes. I have changed my leadership style so that everyone knows what they need to know and how to get there. My mind runs ahead of the game . . . We need to be proactive not reactive, but we have to carefully manage innovation to minimize the workload of, and impact on, the staff.
>
> (Primary head)

This third dilemma reflects the position of many of the headteachers in the study as they found themselves caught between two sets of imperatives for changes – internal and external. The external impetus for change was the 'imposed' changes (e.g. DfEE, Ofsted or the LEA):

> Changes are externally imposed so that the head must interpret incoming documents before she can inform the staff. The speed with which those changes have had to be introduced means that she has had little time to motivate staff

and she is finding it increasingly difficult to justify imposing yet more demands for change.

(Infant deputy)

The internal imperatives on the other hand were a complex mixture of school-based factors (e.g. the 'given' needs of a particular school, which would exist irrespective of the type of leadership approach adopted – the level of staff competence and motivation, the culture of the school and the current level of pupil achievement) and the leadership approaches of the head-teachers as they tried to establish a particular vision, values framework or school ethos:

Leadership is about getting across to the staff where we are now and where we are going so that they can see what the head wants.

(Secondary teacher)

I enjoy being the leader, the autonomy, the finger in every pie, and take pride in moving the school forward and achieving the aims.

(Primary head)

There are inevitable tensions concerning how best to manage externally imposed change within a school. If headteachers over-prescribe what is to happen they can be accused of presenting staff with a *fait accompli* or 'railroading' them. On the other hand, if they under-prepare staff for change they can be seen as being reactive, rushing things through too quickly:

She's a good leader but she's a better manager, because she's doing things yesterday. She does things yesterday and we have to, or I have to, get her to do them tomorrow. She is extremely quick and she expects everybody else's brain to be as quick as hers. To me a leader will be quick but they will allow everybody else, give everybody time, to get on the ship. She wants you on the ship and around the world before you've got your passport sorted . . . She can't understand why everyone else isn't as independent as her. She will have fifteen things going on at the same time and she will have her finger on every single one of them. I couldn't do that. I am a bit more methodical.

(Infant deputy)

The challenge of adapting and customizing external imperatives to the needs of a school becomes a leadership dilemma when heads can no longer justify such changes in terms of the needs of their school:

> I don't mind taking decisions as long as they are sensible ones. I dislike taking decisions that are imposed from outside and that are not useful to the school.
>
> (Secondary head)

> There is nothing more important than the pupils in the school, no budget, not Ofsted, nothing. They are what we are here for and their well-being and success is of paramount importance.
>
> (Secondary head)

The clash between externally imposed changes and internal needs or the values of staff moves from being a management issue and becomes a dilemma when it presents headteachers with the choice of having to adopt the role of either 'subcontractor' or 'subversive'. As subcontractors they become one more link in a chain leading down from those who have developed a policy through its various stages of implementation until it impacts on teachers and pupils. The limit that this role places on their autonomy and decision making, combined with the visibility and public nature of their loss of control, is likely to undermine their moral authority as leaders as they seek to justify the unjustifiable. The role of the subversive, on the other hand, may raise issues of duplicity and intrigue, which may tarnish their moral lead within the school. The heads in this study were neither subcontractors nor subversives, but, with integrity, they skilfully mediated external changes so that they integrated with the vision and values which existed in the schools.

Conclusion

The seven tensions and three dilemmas presented here highlight the complex and fraught nature of headship. They illustrate that effective heads, like others, must manage these while engaging in the central tasks of building cultures and promoting learning and achievement. Indeed, they are an inherent part of the context in which these occur. There are no easy or perfect answers. The worlds of schools, like those of classrooms, hold too many variables and few neat solutions. The concepts are useful because they reveal that effective leaders are not always successful at all times with all people and that a key characteristic is their determination and ability to continue to try to reconcile the irreconcilable.

8

POST-TRANSFORMATIONAL LEADERSHIP

This final chapter considers the characteristics of effective leadership now and in the foreseeable future. While firm conclusions cannot be drawn from a study of only 12 headteachers, the rich source of data they have provided, together with the perceptions of a range of stakeholders, does, we believe, offer a powerful and authentic range of insights into the realities of effective leadership in schools as they enter the new millennium. The chapter will begin by reviewing the relationship between leadership and school improvement. It will argue that the widespread use of bureaucratic leadership and entrepreneurial leadership has not improved schools in the ways intended. The evidence is sufficient to suggest that existing rational theories of leadership do not adequately reflect or explain the current practice of effective leaders. Rather, this reveals a people-centred model of leadership that is premised upon values rather than management systems and market forces. The chapter will explore the dimensions of a 'new' model of leadership more appropriate to purposes and needs. This has been called **'values-led contingency leadership'**.

As the previous chapters have shown, the emerging picture of school leadership in the late 1990s in all countries has become increasingly complex. In England, the pace of change shows no sign of slackening as the government continues to impose new demands upon schools and to expect results within relatively short timescales. Much of the impetus for implementing successive national reforms rests primarily with the leaders of individual institutions. As a consequence, headteachers are increasingly being viewed as 'managing directors', publicly accountable for improving the performance of their school in ways which are measurable (Teacher Training Agency 1999).

> We know that effective teaching must be supported by high-quality management and leadership at middle and senior levels in the profession . . . Managers and leaders also need to be accountable for progress, at whatever level they manage.
> (Teacher Training Agency 1996: 9)

While the development of effective leadership within education is both necessary and desirable, it has been argued that the particular view of leadership which the nature, direction and pace of reform implicitly endorses as effective has become increasingly managerialist (Gunter 1997; Slee *et al.* 1998). Ball (1987) argues that the dominant discourse of leadership embodies a mixture of direct control ('old managerialism') and so-called people-centred management ('new managerialism'). As Mahony and Hextall (1997) point out, a flavour of this can be detected from the first two key areas of headship as identified in the National Standards for Headteachers. In the section on 'Strategic Direction and Development', heads 'lead', 'provide inspiration and motivation', 'create', 'implement', 'ensure', 'monitor', 'evaluate', 'review' and take 'necessary action'. In the section on 'Teaching and Learning' they 'create and maintain', 'determine, organise and implement' and 'monitor and evaluate (Teacher Training Agency 1997: 6–7). This presents a model of headship as being predominantly hierarchical and management-orientated. However, there is evidence from this research study, and from a growing literature on the subject, that this model fails to capture the complexity of leadership and the means by which leaders may become effective and maintain effectiveness within the current post-transformational educational climate.

Glatter's comments encapsulate this point:

> We in 'mainstream' educational management have become too preoccupied with what might be called the institutional side of leadership and management to the extent of

disregarding, or at least under-emphasising, policy and contextual factors. In doing so we may be playing into the hands of those who accuse educational management of being too technocratic and mechanistic and of paying insufficient regard to values.

(Glatter *et al.* 1996: 3)

The findings from the research study on which this book is based have demonstrated that effective leadership is defined and driven by individual value systems, rather than instrumental managerial concerns. They demonstrate also the important influences of social, political, economic and personal and professional contexts on effective leadership. Moreover, they illustrate that there are alternative models to the bureaucratic, rational and entrepreneurial forms of leadership espoused in government policy and documentation which are more appropriate to leaders in the new millennium and more likely to lead to success. Thus, they pose a direct challenge to the current orthodoxy of such forms of leadership theory and leadership training which are based upon them.

Leadership and school improvement

Research findings from diverse countries and different school contexts have revealed the powerful impact of leadership on processes related to school effectiveness and improvement (e.g. Van Velzen *et al.* 1985; Ainscow *et al.* 1994; Hopkins *et al.* 1994; Stoll and Fink 1996). Essentially, schools that are effective and have the capacity to improve are led by headteachers who make a significant and measurable contribution to the effectiveness of their staff. Whatever else is disputed about this complex area of activity, the centrality of leadership in the achievement of school effectiveness and school improvement remains unequivocal.

This broadening of interest in, and understanding of, the leadership role parallels the pattern of development of leadership theory generally. Chapter 3 charted an increasing emphasis within school development upon the links between leadership and the culture of the organization (Dalin 1996) and a move away from the notion of leadership as a series of transactions within a given cultural context towards a view of leadership as transformational, having the potential to alter the cultural context in which teachers teach and students learn. This leadership perspective focuses on the moral values and value-laden activities of leaders and how these are disclosed to other colleagues. It is this perspective that led Hodgkinson (1991) and Sergiovanni (1992) to describe leadership as a 'moral art' rather than a technical science. Implicit in this view is also the notion of shared or devolved leadership activity where leadership is not only the preserve of the headteacher. This blends well with the micropolitical focus of the work of Blase and Anderson (1995) who argue that leaders acting in this mode try to use power with, or through, other people, rather than exercising control over them. Indeed, research evidence into effective schools demonstrates that promoting a more dynamic and decentralized approach to leadership is associated with school improvement. Recent reassessment of the leadership role of the headteacher implies that giving others real responsibility and developing others is the best possible way of moving the organization forward. This means relinquishing the idea of structure as control and replacing it with a view of structure as the vehicle for building the learning capacities of others in the organization.

In relation to this, the importance of mobilizing development at school level, department level and classroom level has been shown to be essential in successful school improvement programmes (e.g. Hopkins *et al.* 1996; Hopkins and Harris 1997). Recent research has shown that a substantial proportion of the variation in effectiveness among schools is due to variation within schools, emphasizing, in secondary schools, the importance of exploring differential effectiveness particularly at the level of the department (Creemers 1992; Scheerens 1992; Harris *et al.* 1996; Sammons *et al.* 1996; Harris 1998), and the importance of devolved leadership at different levels within the organization (Fullan 1992a, b; Hopkins *et al.* 1994, 1997b). Although schools need to be led by individuals (who do make a difference), that overarching leadership has to be replicated right through the organization and found in every aspect of school life.

Yet, there is also research evidence suggesting that there is an ever-growing divide between 'leaders' and 'followers' as a result of the changes arising from the self-governance of all schools (Wallace and Hall 1994). The strong managerialist culture apparent in many schools has reinforced the separateness of the senior management team and has claimed leadership as an activity for the few, rather than the many. The fact that headteachers have the ultimate responsibility for human, financial and other resources inevitably encourages division rather than cohesion. One of the major challenges for headteachers, therefore, is to lead in ways that break down such barriers rather than contribute to their creation or reinforcement.

It has been claimed that the emphasis upon the 'monitorial' role of 'chief executive' (Hughes 1985) has given heads less time to perform the role of 'leading professional' (Pollard *et al.* 1994). This claim directly contrasts with the popular view that the headteacher's main role is to influence the quality of teaching and learning in the school through purposeful 'transformative leadership' (Leithwood and Jantzi 1990; Fullan 1992b). Yet neither the 'monitorial' nor the 'transformative' nor the 'transactional' roles exactly match the leadership behaviours of heads in this study. It was clear, for example, that the heads did not use exchange and rewards as a means of motivating and controlling others but adhered to a 'person-centred' philosophy that placed emphasis upon improving teaching and learning via high expectations of others. For them, the primary task of leadership concerned building and monitoring the conditions for professional, institutional and broader community growth (Leithwood *et al.* 1999).

Within the study, there was also ample evidence that people were trusted to work as autonomous professionals, within clear collegial value frameworks which were common to all. There was a strong emphasis upon teamwork and participation in decision making (though heads reserved the right to be autocratic). Goals were clear and agreed, communications were good and everyone had high expectations of themselves and others. These collegial cultures were maintained, however, within contexts of organizational and individual accountability set by external policy demands and internal aspirations. These created ongoing tensions and dilemmas which had to be managed and mediated as part of the establishment and maintenance of effective leadership cultures. These heads, for example, were able to live with the dilemmas of 'develop or dismiss', 'subcontracting or mediation' or 'power over or power with'. They were not part of, nor did they encourage, a 'dependency' culture (Fullan 1998). They were constantly engaged with the daily business of simultaneously managing interpersonal relations and challenging others to give of their best in the context of policy-driven imperatives which were not always universally welcomed. The heads achieved this by communicating to others a clear vision and set of values. They had been able to raise the self-confidence, morale and sense of achievement of staff by developing a climate of collaboration and by applying high standards to themselves and others. Their focus was always upon the betterment of the children, young people and staff who worked in their schools. In this respect, they exercised 'educative leadership' (Duignan and McPherson 1992). They were empathetic, warm, genuine in their love for children and concerned for their well-being and achievement (Noddings 1992; Jackson *et al.* 1993; Mintzberg 1994). All valued and encouraged collegiality, a feature of 'moving' schools (Rosenholtz 1989; Hargreaves 1991), and all fostered climates of openness in their schools between students, staff and community, encouraging staff to participate in discussions about values and beliefs as well as in decision-making processes, emphasizing mutual respect and providing supportive leadership for all their staff.

In short, they led both the cognitive and the affective lives of the school, combining structural (developing clear goals), political (building alliances) and educational leadership (professional development and teaching improvement) with symbolic leadership (presence, inspiration) and human 'principle-centred' leadership (demonstrating care and support) (Bolman and Deal 1984; Covey 1990). However, it was the human resource management which occupied most of their daily time and which created the most tensions and celebration. In this respect, their leadership approaches were heavily people-centred. They were both transactional – ensuring that systems were maintained and developed, targets were formulated and met and that their schools ran smoothly – and transformative – building on esteem, competence, autonomy and achievement, raising 'the level of human conduct and ethical aspiration of both the leader and the led' (Sergiovanni 1992); and bonding, 'by inspiring extraordinary commitment and performance' (Sergiovanni 1992: 25). In these schools, a new kind of hierarchy had emerged: 'one that places purposes, values and commitments at the apex and teachers, principals, parents and students below in service to these purposes ...' (Sergiovanni 1992: 27).

It seems that morality, emotion and social bonds provide far more powerful stimulants to motivation and commitment than the extrinsic concerns of transactional leadership in which leaders and followers exchange needs and services to achieve independent objectives. Sergiovanni's (1995) concepts of 'servant leadership' and 'stewardship' and the 'flexibility' and 'resiliency' which he sees as key characteristics of effective leaders relate closely to the findings in this study, as does the work in England by Grace (1995) and Bottery (1992) which focuses upon the ethics of leadership:

> Leadership in general must maintain an ethical focus which is oriented towards democratic values within a community. This has to do with the meaning of ethics historically – as a search for the good life of a community . . . Ethics here refers to a more comprehensive construct than just individual behaviour; rather it implicates us and how we as a moral community live our communal lives.
>
> (Grace 1995: 55)

The heads in this study operated on the basis of both internally and externally determined measures of quality control so that their quality assurance criteria had a broader agenda in keeping with a holistic broader moral vision of a good school and good teachers. It involved everyone in the organization seeking systematically, with evidence, to ensure that standards were constantly improving. It was contingent but within a framework of unshakeable core values. All the heads:

- were clear in their vision for the school and communicated it to all its constituents;
- focused upon care and achievement simultaneously;
- created, maintained and constantly monitored relationships, recognizing them as key to the cultures of learning;
- were reflective in a variety of internal and external social and organizational contexts, using a variety of problem-solving approaches;
- sought, synthesized and evaluated internal and external data, applying these to the school within their values framework;
- persisted with apparently intractable issues in their drive for higher standards;
- were prepared to take risks in order to achieve these;

- were not afraid to ask difficult questions of themselves and others;
- were entrepreneurial;
- were 'networkers' inside and outside the school;
- were not afraid to acknowledge failure but did not give up and learnt from it;
- were aware of a range of sources to help solve problems;
- managed ongoing tensions and dilemmas through principled, values-led contingency leadership.

In research on school leaders in Denmark, Scotland, England and Australia, John MacBeath and his colleagues asked teachers to choose from five definitions of leadership which were closest to and furthest away from their views of an effective leader. The headteachers in this study provided examples of all five, reinforcing the developing notion of core characteristics of effective leaders:

1. Leadership means having a clear personal vision of what you want to achieve.
2. Good leaders are in the thick of things, working alongside their colleagues.
3. Leadership means respecting teachers' autonomy, protecting them from extraneous demands.
4. Good leaders look ahead, anticipate change and prepare people for it so that it doesn't surprise or disempower them.
5. Good leaders are pragmatic. They are able to grasp the realities of the political and economic context and they are able to negotiate and compromise.

(MacBeath 1998: 63)

The evidence from this research confirms these findings and suggests the addition of a sixth definition:

6. Good leaders are informed by, and communicate, clear sets of personal and educational values which represent their moral purposes for the school.

One recent theoretical model of leadership which places an emphasis upon the development of the school through the development of others is the model of 'pedagogical leadership'. Pedagogical leadership is described by Sergiovanni (1998) as that which invests in capacity building by developing social and academic capital for students and intellectual and professional capital for teachers. He argues that this model differs from the existing bureaucratic, visionary and entrepreneurial leadership theories that dominate the literature because it is concerned with adding value by developing various forms of human capital. The heads in the study were centrally concerned with developing their organization through developing others. In Sergiovanni's (1998) analysis they developed social capital by encouraging collegiality and collaboration. The data provided by teachers, pupils, parents and governors emphasized 'building community' as an important dimension of the leadership role. Furthermore, it was evident that within the various school communities there was a strong and clear commitment to academic achievement as evidenced by the heads' high expectations of their staff. This academic capital was developed through a commitment to the success of all pupils and a shared belief in rewarding and praising pupils.

Sergiovanni (1998) points out that within schools professional capital is created as a fabric of reciprocal responsibilities and mutual support. The heads in this study involved others in decision making and had professional trust in them. They cultivated professional dialogue between teachers, placing a high premium upon their own professional development and the professional development of their staff. In this respect, they developed professional and intellectual capital by encouraging their schools to become inquiring communities.

Post-transformational leadership: a values-led contingency model

It is clear that the heads in this study continue to operate effectively in situations in which successive governments have sought to impose policies that largely require a scientific/rational–economic approach to management within schools. However, the evidence is that they are operating quite different forms of leadership to those espoused by government rhetoric. These effective heads, albeit within the results-driven, achievement-oriented demands of government, are more concerned with making their schools caring, focused and inquiring communities than cost-effective quasi-businesses.

The two most important findings from this research are that, first, effective leaders are constantly and consistently managing several competing tensions and dilemmas; and second, effective leaders are, above all, people-centred:

> Managers know that people make the critical difference between success and failure. The effectiveness with which organisations manage, develop, motivate, involve and engage the willing contribution of the people who work in them is a key determinant of how well those organisations perform ... employee commitment and positive 'psychological contact' between employer and employee are fundamental to improving performance.
>
> (Patterson *et al.* 1997: vii–viii)

The research from which this quotation is taken drew upon data gathered from a ten-year ongoing study of over a hundred small and medium-sized manufacturing enterprises in the UK ranging in size from 60 to 1000 employees, averaging 253. While it shares some of the characteristics of other recent research into the relationship over time between people management (Huselid 1995; MacDuffie 1995) and other management practices such as the use of competitive strategies, quality focus and investment in research and development, it studied predominantly single-site and single-product operations. The results showed that no other management practice had such a powerful impact upon performance – whether this was measured in terms of productivity or profitability – as people management. It follows that successful single-site, multi-product operations such as schools would also benefit from placing a great deal of emphasis upon the management of people:

> The more satisfied workers are with their jobs the better the company is likely to perform in terms of subsequent profitability and particularly productivity.
>
> (Patterson *et al.* 1997: x)

The results [of the study] suggest that, if managers wish to influence the performance of their companies, the most important area they should emphasise is the management of people.

> (Patterson *et al.* 1997: xi)

These findings match our own on effective school leadership. In this respect, it is worth examining further the 'competing values' theoretical framework which Patterson and his colleagues (Patterson *et al.* 1997: 9) used to guide their work, for much may be applied to current and future educational contexts:

- **Human relations model** in which 'the primary emphasis is on norms and values associated with belonging, trust and participation. Motivational factors are attachment, cohesiveness and group membership. Cultural dimensions linked to this are: *concern for employee welfare* – the extent to which employees feel valued and trusted; *autonomy* – designing jobs in ways which give employees wide scope to enact work; *emphasis on training* – a concern with developing employee skills; and *supervisory support.*'

- **Open systems model** in which the primary emphasis is on change and innovation, 'where norms and values are associated with growth, resource acquisition and adaptation. Motivational factors are growth, variety, stimulation. Cultural dimensions which reflect this orientation are: *outward forms* – where the organisation is attuned to the external environment; *flexibility; innovation and reviewing objectives* – a concern with reviewing and reflecting upon progress in order to improve.'

- **Rational goal model** in which the primary emphasis is on 'the pursuit and attainment of well-defined objectives, where norms and values are associated with productivity, performance, goal fulfilment and achievement. Motivations are competition and successful achievement of predetermined ends. Cultural dimensions which reflect this model are: *vision* – a concern with clearly defining where the organisation is heading; *emphasis on quality: pressure to produce* – where employees feel pressured to meet targets and deadlines; and *performance feedback* – where clear feedback is available for employees about their job performance.'

- **Internal process model** in which the emphasis is on 'stability, internal organisation and adherence to rules, where norms and values are associated with efficiency, coordination and uniformity. Motivating factors are needs for security, order and rules and regulations. Cultural dimensions which reflect this model are: *formalization* – a concern with formal (often written) rules and procedures; *efficiency*; and *tradition* – a concern with maintaining existing policies, practices and procedures.'

Each of these models will have an effect upon performance, but in terms of their relative importance, the research of Patterson and his colleagues showed the following ranking: human relations, internal process, rational goal and open systems. This order would accord exactly with the relative emphasis provided by all the stakeholders' perceptions of their headteachers. Effective heads, it seems, manage a balance of high levels of concern with the welfare and support of staff with internal stability. As Patterson *et al.* (1997) wrote:

> It is employees within companies who bring about changes in productivity and how they are managed in terms of concern for employee welfare, emphasis on supervisory support, social support, etc., is likely to be critical.
>
> (p. 12)

A number of writers (Blackmore 1989; Shakeshaft 1989) have argued for a paradigm shift in conceptions of leadership which start not from the basis of power and control but from the ability to act with others and to enable others to act. The heads in the study rarely used their authority to drive through change, or to influence others. Instead they used their personal rather than positional power to obtain the results they wanted. Yet at the core of their personal power resided a particular vision for the school shaped by a particular set of values. These effective headteachers saw themselves as the source of a vision for their institutions, working through various processes of consultation, to enlist the support and commitment of staff.

Rosener's (1990) notion of interactive leadership emphasizes the enhancement of self-worth. In her view, it is the approach most likely to meet the demands of the workforce for increased participation, as well as the demands of the economy for flexible and adaptable organizations. Interactive leadership embodies a repertoire of leadership styles that is more representative of the effective leadership practice described in the study. Heads in the study and their constituencies consistently highlighted the importance of possessing a range of leadership strategies to address the diverse sets of issues and problems they faced. They also emphasized the contingent nature of many of the decisions they made and how different leadership strategies would be used in different contexts.

This new model of leadership we are proposing, therefore, takes leadership and management to be mutually reinforcing within a conception of leadership that is diffuse rather than hierarchical. The knowledge and skills that are required are both generic and specific, within and between phases and sectors. The kind of moral leadership that Hodgkinson advocates, for example, is a generic feature of effective leaders. Similarly, effective leaders must have the ability to read and adjust to the particular context or set of circumstances they face. In this respect, their leadership behaviour is contingent on context and situation. The choices they make relate directly to their own beliefs, values and leadership style. Different contexts will present different challenges and will require different responses. In the turbulent and unpredictable climate of uncertain and changing challenges which characterize schools of today and tomorrow the room for manoeuvre is constrained and inevitable tensions arise. Consequently, effective leadership in the twenty-first century will be essentially concerned with adapting strategies and tactics (but not values) to address unanticipated events and new demands.

The capacity of leaders to make a difference will, then, depend upon their interpretation of and responses to the constraints, demands and choices that they face. Goldring (1997) argues that effective leaders, like those in this study, must know how to span boundaries in order to promote information and resource control. At the same time as they negotiate the constraints of internal and external environments, they must capitalize on the many opportunities for making choices.

Values-led contingency leadership

While a case has been made here for the centrality of vision and the leader's role in creating a vision for, and maintaining a vision in, the organization, the art of leading and managing cannot be an entirely rational process. The progression from philosophy to vision to goals and outcomes is rarely linear or logical. While the notion of the self-managing school appears an attractive and pragmatic method of policy making, less easily identified are the knowledge, qualities, skills or competencies that allow leaders to manage and lead successfully.

The concept of leadership proposed here, then, has a number of different dimensions which combine to represent the complexity of leadership. It includes a range of features, or characteristics that are not mutually exclusive.

Values and vision

Centrally important in this new model of leadership is the co-operation, and alignment to the leader's values and vision, of those of others. The heads in the study communicated their personal vision and belief systems by direction, words and deeds. Through a variety of symbolic gestures and action, they were successful at realigning both staff and pupils to their particular vision of the school. As Bhindi and Duignan (1996) have proposed in their visionary paradigm for leadership in 2020:

> Organisations are not solely concerned with outcomes, processes and resources. They are also concerned with the human spirit and their values and relationships. Authentic leaders breathe the life force into the workplace and keep the people feeling energised and focused. As stewards and guides they build people and their self esteeem. They derive their credibility from personal integrity and 'walking' their values.
>
> (Bhindi and Duignan 1996: 29)

Integrity

In many respects, the heads in the study did 'walk the talk'. Through the consistency and integrity of their actions, they modelled behaviour that they considered desirable to achieve the school goals (Caldwell and Spinks 1998). This dimension of values-led contingency leadership incorporates, but is more than, what has been termed by Stoll and Fink (1996) as invitational leadership. This emphasizes the way in which positive and negative interactions shape one's concept of self. Invitations are messages communicated to people which inform them that they are able, responsible and worthwhile. Such messages are communicated through interpersonal action, but also through institutional policies, programmes, practices and physical environments. Invitational leadership is built upon four basic premises:

- *optimism* – the belief that people have untapped potential for growth and development;
- *respect* – the recognition that each person is an individual;
- *trust* – the ability to trust others to behave in concert and in turn, as leaders, to behave with integrity;
- *intention* – the capacity to be actively supportive, caring and encouraging.

All of these were perceived characteristics of the heads in the study which has provided the basis for this book. The heads in the study did display invitational leadership in their day-to-day dealings with individuals. Their behaviour with others was premised upon respect and trust and their belief in developing the potential of staff and students commonly held. Their ability to invite others to share and develop their vision was frequently commented upon by staff and students alike. Alongside these qualities, however, were examples of heads being firm (in relation to values, expectations and standards), and, on occasion, ruthless. In many respects, the way they interacted with others was the common denominator of their success. The human qualities they possessed enabled them to lead others effectively and to establish confidence in others that their vision was worth sharing.

Context

Another important dimension of effective leadership is the power of context. The heads in the study were highly responsive to the demands and challenges within and beyond their own school context. In managing people and cultural change they managed external as well as internal environments. They had skills in communicating, in supporting colleagues' development so that they felt confident in fulfilling expectations of their contribution to the achievement of strategic goals and in the management of conflict and negotiating positive outcomes. In this sense, they were 'adaptive' (Heifetz 1994). In adaptive leadership, first developed in a medical context, it is recognized that the leader's task is to advance the goals of the organization by designing appropriate strategies which others must carry out. However, 'resolving problems' and 'tackling the tough decisions' is seen as a context-related collective responsibility. Thus the role of the leader is to engage in activities designed to raise awareness, or 'ripen the issues' in order to mobilize groups to tackle the issues and to take responsibility for consequences of their decisions (Edwards 1999). The heads in the study were adaptive and through these processes were able to manage conflict in a way that achieved positive outcomes. They were also adept at keeping the balance between involving others and taking individual action. It is clear, then, that effective leaders are able, within competing values frameworks, to combine a moral purpose with a willingness to be collaborative and to promote collaboration among colleagues, whether through teamwork, or extending the boundaries of participation in decision making.

Continuing professional development: power with and through

The heads in this study adopted highly creative approaches to tackling the complex demands of implementing multiple change. The decision to work with and through teams as well as individuals was a common response to the management of change. Telford (1996) argues that collaborative leadership is the most certain way of ensuring the vision of the school is realized. Her model of collaborative leadership identifies 'artistry' as an additional key ingredient of successful school leadership. Such artistry is required to read the idiosyncrasies of each leadership context and to know how to exploit the situation to maximum advantage. Within the study the heads did operate a form of collaborative leadership and saw staff and students as central to achieving the school's purpose. The heads used a number of strategies for bringing out the best in staff. In addition to formal development opportunities, these strategies included the power of praise; involving others in decision making; giving professional autonomy; leading by standing behind, alongside and in front. Although the heads tended to concentrate on teaching staff in the first instance, they used similar approaches when dealing with governors, parents and, to some extent, students. All the heads invested in others in order to lead the school. From the perspectives of governors, deputies, teachers, parents and pupils the overarching message was one of the head building the community of the school in its widest sense, i.e. through developing and involving others.

Reflection: developing the self

Teachers' work in many countries is increasingly being directed by closely monitored government policy initiatives, suggesting that only 'technical' reflection – a relatively simple form of practice evaluation – is necessary. Many heads still rely mainly upon experience and intuition – with all the limitations to change which these contain – to guide them through their careers. The evidence from this research suggests, however, that good heads are those who move beyond intuition, learning from experience, and technical reflection, and encourage their teachers to do the same. In this study heads saw themselves as having a responsibility for the education of teachers and students which went beyond the instrumental, encompassing responsibilities to educate for citizenship and to imbue in their students a positive disposition towards lifelong learning.

Underpinning this model of values-led contingency leadership, either implicitly or explicitly, was the heads' capacity to be reflective in different ways about their own values, beliefs and practices and those of their staff; the position and progress of their schools in relation to others in local and national contexts; current and emerging policy matters which affected management and the curriculum; and conditions of service for teachers in their schools. The research suggests that such capacity for reflection in, on and about a broad range of contexts, and through this to form, sustain, review and renew a holistic view of the school, its needs and its direction, is central to effective professional leadership. For these heads also, effective leadership was as much about developing the self as about capacity building in others. Effective leadership required an intelligent head with an intelligent heart. It required heads to engage *simultaneously* in reflection in, on and about the action in each context in which they work. Reflection upon practice, then, was not related to hierarchical levels identified by Handal (1990), van Manen (1977) and Carr and Kemmis (1986). Rather, such technical, practical and emancipatory forms of reflection were interactive and heads used each differentially according to circumstance and purpose. Effective heads in this study were, in fact, *critical thinkers* who had developed an awareness of the assumptions under which they and others think and behave. They were sceptical of 'quick fix' solutions to problems:

When we think critically, we ... refuse to relinquish the
responsibility for making the choices that determine our
individual and collective futures ... We become actively
engaged in creating our personal and social worlds ... We
take the reality of democracy seriously ...

(Brookfield 1987: ix, x)

However, such critical thinking was underpinned by a recognition of the power of the heart as well as the head in influencing
beliefs and practices.

This ability to recognize emotions in others, handle relationships, manage emotions and know one's own emotions has been
defined as *'emotional intelligence'* (Goleman 1995), which is fundamental to effective leadership. The empirical evidence from this
study clearly endorses emotional intelligence as a legitimate part
of effective leadership.

The future of leadership development

Within the realms of professional development and training, the
current orthodoxy is still inherently managerialist and rational.
Although it is outside the remit of this book to engage in an
in-depth critique of current training provision, it is important to
consider how far the existing training models either reflect or
promote effective leadership. An analysis of the main training
programmes for headteachers quickly reveals a common theoretical and ideological position concerning leadership training.
HEADLAMP, the National Professional Qualification for Headteachers (NPQH) and the Leadership Programme for Serving
Headteachers (LPSH) (TTA 1998) are premised upon a human
resource management model, which has its origins in business
organizations rather than schools. As a consequence, the models
of leadership espoused in these training routes are inherently
normative, rational and managerialist. There is little scope within
the competency-based training model, or the formulaic training
package, to explore those dimensions of emotional intelligence
that have been shown to contribute significantly to effective
leadership. Instead, leadership is presented in a relatively unpro-
blematic and uniform way, thus reinforcing a view that the aim
of the leader is to bring order and control through the exercise
of rational processes.

Effective leaders have been shown to be reflective, caring and highly principled people who emphasize the human dimension of the management enterprise. They place a high premium upon personal values and are more concerned with cultural rather than structural change. They have moved beyond a narrow rational, managerial view of their role to a more holistic, value-led approach guided by personal experience and professional preference.

It is within this context that competency-driven accreditation and training initiatives for headteachers need to be examined. The rapid adaptation and adoption of the managerial model within the current approaches to training excludes other versions of organizational life from headteacher development (Gunter 1997). As a consequence, it is questionable whether such forms of training can facilitate the development of knowledge necessary for the type of leadership practice that is effective. Given the weight of evidence from this study concerning the centrality of personal values, self-awareness and interpersonal skill proficiency within effective leadership practice, and the relative absence of this within training programmes, the prognosis remains poor.

Even the most recent training programmes fail to address the key themes that have emerged from the study. If the needs of those aspiring, new and experienced heads who wish to become and remain successful in the changing times of the twenty-first century are to be met, then programmes must focus upon:

- analysis of personal and professional values, central to successful leadership;
- critical, reflective thinking;
- promotion of people-centred continuing professional development as a means of maintaining and raising levels of commitment and morale (echoing Roland Barth's wise dictum that heads must be the 'leading learners' in their schools);
- emphasis upon intra as well as inter personal skill development;
- recognition of the importance to successful learning and achievement of attending to the emotional as well as the cognitive mind;
- problem solving and the management of 'competing forces' – key components of leadership training for school improvement if schools are to become the high achieving learning communities espoused by government.

Currently, there is no coherent set of programmes which addresses the development of such key leadership qualities and skills. Yet such training and development cannot be left to chance. Perhaps one of the primary tasks for the National College for School Leadership in England will be to ensure that expertise from appropriate fields of education and business is used to develop programmes that are based upon the real needs of heads attempting to exercise successful leadership in changing times.

Within governments' overall strategic vision for education in all countries, the training, reskilling and certification of heads occupies a central place. The problem is that many of the training models focus upon managerial rather than leadership functions. In doing so they fail to build capacities of heads to reflect upon their own values and those of the whole school community and do not place sufficient emphasis upon building the range of interpersonal qualities and skills necessary and appropriate to effective leadership. For governments' rhetoric of lifelong learning, high teaching standards, pupil achievement and school improvement to become a reality, schools need to be led by headteachers who are not only knowledgeable and skilled in managerial techniques but also, like those in this study, people-centred leaders who are able to combine the management of internal and external change with a strong development and achievement orientation. Their practices need to be based upon clear and communicated values to which all in their community subscribe.

If schools are to become 'knowledge creating' in which 'the knowledge of all the school's members and partners is recognised' and shared (Hargreaves 1998: 29), if teachers are to continue to be committed to making a difference in the learning lives of their students through skilful teaching combined with the ethics of 'care, justice and inclusiveness' (Hargreaves and Fullan 1998: 35), then effective headteachers may themselves be justifiably expected to demonstrate these qualities through the kinds of leadership they exercise.

Power and politics will continue to provide the context and daily realities for life in all schools and it is the management of the tensions and dilemmas that these create which, within a strong values framework, is a distinguishing feature of effective leadership. The heads in this study were effective because they held and communicated clear vision and values. They empowered staff by developing a climate of collaboration, by applying high standards to themselves and others and monitoring these, by seeking the support of various influential groups within the school community, by keeping 'ahead of the game' through ensuring that they had a national strategic view of forthcoming changes, and by managing their own personal and professional selves. They managed tensions between dependency and autonomy, between caution and courage, between maintenance and development. In mediating between their own moral framework and those of the communities in which they worked, their focus was always upon the betterment of the young people and staff who worked in their schools. They remained also, often against all the odds, enthusiastic and committed to learning. Their strength was demonstrated in their hopefulness at all times, for:

> Hope is definitely not the same thing as optimism. It is not the conviction that something will turn out well, but the certainty that something makes sense, regardless of how it turns out. It is hope, above all, that gives us strength to live and to continually try new things, even in conditions that seem hopeless.
>
> (Havel 1993: 68)

REFERENCES

Acker, S. (1990) Teachers' culture in an English primary school: continuity and change, *British Journal of Sociology of Education*, 11 (3): 257–73.

Ainscow, M., Hopkins, D., Southworth, G. and West, M. (1994) *Creating the Conditions for School Improvement*. London: David Fulton.

Ainscow, M. and Southworth, G. (1995) School improvement: a study of the roles of leaders and external consultants. Mimeo, University of Cambridge Institute of Education.

Andersson, B-E. (1996) Why am I in school? A study of Swedish adolescents' perceptions of their school situation, *EERA Bulletin*, July: 17–23.

Babad, E., Bernieri, F. and Rosenthal, R. (1991) Students as judges of teachers' verbal and non-verbal behaviour, *American Educational Research Journal*, 28 (1): 211–34.

Ball, S. (1987) *The Micropolitics of the School: Towards a Theory of School Organisation*. London: Methuen.

Barrow, R. (1976) Competence and the head, in R.S. Peters (ed.) *The Role of the Head*. London: Routledge and Kegan Paul.

Barth, R.S. (1990a) *Improving Schools from Within: Teachers, Parents and Principals Can Make the Difference*. San Francisco: Jossey-Bass.

Barth, R.S. (1990b) A personal vision of a good school, *Phi Delta Kappan*, March: 512–16.

Barth, R.S. (1996) Building a community of learners. South Bay School Leadership Team Development Seminar Series: Seminar 10, California, California School Leadership Center.

Bass, B.M. and Avolio, B.J. (1993) Transformational leadership: a response to critiques, in M.M. Chemers (ed.) *Leadership Theory and Research Perspectives and Directions*. San Diego: Academic Press.

Beck, L.G. and Murphy, J. (1993) *Understanding the Principalship: Metaphorical Themes 1920s–1990s*. New York: Teachers College Press.

Beresford, J. (1997) Ask the children, *Reading*, 31 (1): 17–18.

Berlak, H. and Berlak, A. (1981) *Dilemmas of Schooling: Teaching and Social Change*. London: Methuen.

Bernbaum, G. (1976) The role of the head, in R.S. Peters (ed.) *The Role of the Head*. London: Routledge and Kegan Paul.

Bhindi, N. and Duignan, P. (1996) Leadership 2020: a visionary paradigm. Paper presented at Commonwealth Council for Educational Administration International Conference, Kuala Lumpur.

Blackmore, J. (1989) 'Educational leadership: a feminist critique and reconstruction', in J. Smyth (ed.) *Critical Perspectives on Educational Leadership*. London: Falmer.

Blase, J. (1989) The micropolitics of the school: the everyday political orientation of teachers toward open school principals, *Educational Administration Quarterly*, 24 (4): 377–407.

Blase, J. and Anderson, G. (1995) *The Micropolitics of Educational Leadership*. London: Cassell.

Blum, R.E. (1997) Learning what students think about school restructuring, in Restructuring Collaborative, *Look Who's Talking Now. Student Views of Learning in Restructured Schools*. Portland: Regional Educational Laboratory Network.

Boisot, M. (1995) Preparing for turbulence: the changing relationship between strategy and management development in the learning organisation, in B. Garratt (ed.) *Developing Strategic Thought*. London: McGraw-Hill.

Bolam, R. (1975) The management of educational change: towards a conceptual framework, in V. Houghton, R. McHugh and C. Morgan (eds) *The Management of Organisations and Individuals*. Buckingham: Open University Press.

Bolman, L.G. and Deal, T.E. (1984) *Modern Approaches to Understanding and Managing Organisations*. San Francisco: Jossey-Bass.

Bottery, M. (1992) *The Ethics of Educational Management: Personal, Social and Political Perspectives on School Organisation*. London: Cassell.

Bottery, M.P. (1988) Educational management: an ethical critique, *Oxford Review of Education*, 14 (3).

Bowe, R. and Ball, S. with Gold, A. (1992) *Reforming Education and Changing Schools: Case Studies in Policy Sociology*. London: Routledge.

Boyd, B. and Jardine, S. (1997) 'Sometimes our views get lost'. Listening to young people talking about school. Paper presented at BERA Conference, York, September.

Boyd, B. and Reeves, J. (1996) Listening to children's voices. Paper presented at BERA Conference, Lancaster, September.

Brandes, D. and Ginnis, P. (1990) *The Student-centred School: Ideas for Practical Visionaries*. Oxford: Blackwell.

Brookfield, S. (1987) *Developing Critical Thinkers: Challenging Adults to Explore Alternative Ways of Thinking and Acting*. New York: Teachers College Press.

Bullock, A. and Thomas, H. (1997) *Schools at the Centre? A Study of Decentralisation*. London: Routledge.

Burgess, R.G. (1988) A headteacher at work during the teachers' dispute. Paper presented at the Histories and Ethnographies of Teachers' Conference, St Hilda's College, Oxford, 12–14 September.

Burns, J.M. (1978) *Leadership*. New York: Harper and Row.

Bush, T. (1986) *Theories of Educational Management*. London: Harper and Row.

Caldwell, B.J. (1997) Rethinking the work of school leaders in an age of change. Paper presented to the 6th National Conference in Educational Research, University of Oslo, Norway, 20–2 May.

Caldwell, B.J. (1999) Reinventing school leadership for lasting reform in the third millennium, in C. Day, A. Fernandez, T.E. Hauge and J. Møller (eds) *The Life and Work of Teachers: International Perspectives in Changing Times*. London: Falmer.

Caldwell, B.J. and Spinks, J.M. (1992) *Leading the Self-Managing School*. London: Falmer.

Caldwell, B.J. and Spinks, J.M. (1998) *Beyond the Self-Managing School*. London: Falmer.

Carr, W. and Kemmis, S. (1986) *Becoming Critical: Knowing through Action Research*. London: Falmer.

Centre for Successful Schools, University of Keele (1990) *Pupil Survey of School Life*, Questionnaire. Keele: University of Keele.

Clarke, J. (1995) The role of the headteacher in school improvement. Mimeo, Suffolk County Council.

Colegate, H.A. (1976) The role of the secondary head, in R.S. Peters (ed.) *The Role of the Head*. London: Routledge and Kegan Paul.

Coleman, P. and Collinge, J. (1998) The good teacher: a student perspective. Paper presented at International Congress on School Effectiveness and School Improvement, Manchester, January.

Consortium on Chicago School Research (1996) *Charting Reform in Chicago: The Students Speak*. Chicago: Consortium on Chicago School Research.

Cooper, P. and Fielding, M. (1998) The issue of student voice. Paper presented at International Congress on School Effectiveness and School Improvement, Manchester, January.

Coopers and Lybrand (1988) *Local Management of Schools*. London: HMSO.

Coulson, A.A. (1976) The role of the primary head, in R.S. Peters (ed.) *The Role of the Head*. London: Routledge and Kegan Paul.

Covey, S.R. (1990) *Principle-centred Leadership*. New York: Summit Books.

Creemers, B. (1992) *The Effective Classroom*. London: Cassell.

Dalin, P. (1996) *School Culture*. London: Cassell.

Davies, B. (1989) Budgetary and economic perspectives and their applications in local management of schools, in B. Fidler and G. Bowles (eds) *Effective Local Management of Schools*. Harlow: Longman, in association with BEMAS (British Educational Management and Administration Society).

Davies, B. and Ellison, L. (1995) Improving the quality of schools – ask the clients?, *School Organisation*, 15 (1): 5–12.

Day, C. and Bakioğlu, A. (1996) Development and disenchantment in the professional lives of headteachers, in I.F. Goodson and A. Hargreaves (eds) *Teachers' Professional Lives*. London: Falmer.

Day, C., Hall, C. and Whitaker, P. (1998) *Developing Leadership in Primary Schools*. London: Paul Chapman.

Day, C., Whitaker, P. and Johnston, D. (1993) *Managing Primary Schools in the 1990s: A Professional Development Approach*. London: Paul Chapman.

Deal, T. and Kennedy, A. (1984) *Corporate Cultures: The Rites and Rituals of Corporate Life*. Reading, MA: Addison Wesley.

Dempster, N. and Mahoney, P. (1998) Ethical challenges in school leadership, in J. MacBeath (ed.) *Effective School Leadership: Responding to Change*. London: Paul Chapman.

Dennison, W. (1988) Top heavy, *Times Educational Supplement*, 3 June.

DES (Department of Education and Science) (1990) *Developing School Management. The Way Forward*. London: HMSO.

DfEE (Department for Education and Employment) (1997) *Excellence in Schools*, CM3681. London: The Stationery Office.

Drever, E. (1995) *Using Semi-Structured Interviews in Small-Scale Research*. Edinburgh: Scottish Council for Research in Education.

Duignan, P.A. and Macpherson, R.J.S. (1992) *Educative Leadership: A Practical Theory for New Administrators and Managers*. London: Falmer.

Earley, P. (1998) Governing bodies and school inspection: potential for empowerment?, in P. Earley (ed.) *School Improvement* after *Inspection?* London: Paul Chapman.

Edwards, J. (1999) Leadership: what AERA needs now, *Professional Education Researcher Quarterly*, 20 (2): 1–6.

Eraut, M.E. (1994) *Developing Professional Knowledge and Competence*. London: Falmer.

Evetts, J. (1993) LMS and headship: changing the contexts for micropolitics, *Educational Review*, 45 (1): 53–65.

Evetts, J. (1994) The new headteacher: the changing work culture of secondary headship, *School Organisation*, 14 (1): 37–47.

Fernandez, D.W. (1986) *Persuasions and Performances: The Play of Tropes in Culture.* Bloomington, IN: Indiana University Press.

Flutter, J., Kershner, R. and Rudduck, J. (1998) *Thinking about Learning, Talking about Learning. A Report of the Effective Learning Project.* Cambridge: Cambridgeshire County Council and Homerton College.

Fullan, M.G. (1992a) *Successful School Improvement.* Buckingham: Open University Press.

Fullan, M.G. (1992b) *What's Worth Fighting for in Headship?* Buckingham: Open University Press.

Fullan, M.G. (1992c) *The New Meaning of Educational Change.* London: Cassell.

Fullan, M.G. (1998) Leadership for the twenty first century: breaking the bonds of dependency, *Educational Leadership*, 55 (7): 6–10.

Gardner, H. (1995) *Leading Minds: An Anatomy of Leadership.* London: Harper Collins.

Gill, J. and Johnson, P. (1991) *Research Methods for Managers.* London: Paul Chapman.

Gipps, C. and Tunstall, P. (1997) Effort, ability and the teacher: young children's explanations for success and failure. Paper presented at the British Educational Research Association (BERA) Annual Conference, York, September.

Glaser, B.G. and Strauss, A.L. (1967) *The Discovery of Grounded Theory: Strategies for Qualitative Research.* Chicago: Aldine Publishing Company.

Glatter, R., Woods, P.A. and Bagley, C. (eds) (1996) *Choice and Diversity in Schooling: Perspectives and Prospects.* London: Routledge.

Gold, K. (1990) Salesmen queue at the head's study, *Observer*, 22 April.

Goldring, E. (1997) Educational leadership: schools, environments and boundary spanning, in M. Preedy *et al.* (eds) *Educational Management Strategy, Quality and Resources.* Buckingham: Open University Press.

Goleman, D. (1995) *Emotional Intelligence.* New York: Bantam Books.

Grace, G. (1995) *School Leadership: Beyond Education Management. An Essay in Policy Scholarship.* Lewes: Falmer.

Gray, J. and Wilcox, B. (1995) *Good School, Bad School: Evaluating Performance and Encouraging Improvement.* Buckingham: Open University Press.

Gunter, H. (1997) *Rethinking Education: The Consequences of Jurassic Management.* London: Cassell.

Hallinger, P. and Heck, R.H. (1996) The principal's role in school effectiveness: an assessment of substantive findings, 1980–1995. Paper presented at the American Educational Research Association (AERA) Annual Conference, New York.

Hallinger, P. and Murphy, J. (1985) Defining an organisational mission in schools. Paper presented at the Annual Meeting of the American Educational Research Association, Chicago, April.

Hammersley, M. and Atkinson, P. (1983) *Ethnography: Principles in Practice*. London: Tavistock.

Handal, G. (1990) Promoting the articulation of tacit knowledge through the counselling of practitioners. Keynote paper at Amsterdam Pedagogisch Centrum Conference, Amsterdam, 6–8 April.

Hargreaves, A. (1992) Cultures of teaching: a focus for change, in A. Hargreaves and M.G. Fullan (eds) *Understanding Teacher Development*. New York: Teachers College Press.

Hargreaves, A. (1994) *Changing Teachers, Changing Times: Teachers' Work and Culture in the Postmodern Age*. New York: Teachers College Press.

Hargreaves, A. and Dawe, R. (1990) Paths of professional development: continued collegiality, collaborative culture, and the case of peer coaching, *Teaching and Teacher Education*, 6 (3): 227–41.

Hargreaves, A. and Fullan, M. (1998) *What's Worth Fighting for Out There*. New York: Teachers College Press.

Hargreaves, D. (1997) A road to the learning society, *School Leadership and Management*, 17 (1): 20.

Hargreaves, D. (1998) *Creative Professionalism: The Role of Teachers in the Knowledge Society*. London: Demos.

Harris, A. (1998) Improving ineffective departments in secondary schools: strategies for change and development, *Educational Management and Administration*, 26 (3): 169–85.

Harris, A., Jamieson, I.M. and Russ, J. (1996) 'What makes an effective department?', *Management in Education*, 10: 7–9.

Harrison, P. (1987) The head was in his counting house . . . , *Times Educational Supplement*, 9 October.

Havel, V. (1993) Never hope against hope, *Esquire*, October: 65–9.

Hayes, L.F. and Ross, D.D. (1989) Trust versus control: the impact of school leadership on teacher reflection, *International Journal of Qualitative Studies in Education*, 2 (4): 335–50.

Heifetz, R.A. (1994) *Leadership without Easy Answers*. Cambridge, MA: Belnap Press.

Heller, H. (1985) *Helping Schools Change. A Handbook for Leaders in Education*. York: Centre for the Study of Comprehensive Schools, York University.

Heywood, J. (1986) Local financial management is on the move in Cambridgeshire, *Education*, 11 April: 340–1.

Hodgkinson, C. (1991) *Educational Leadership: The Moral Art*. Albany, NY: State University of New York Press.

Hodgkinson, C. (1993) *The Philosophy of Leadership*. Oxford: Basil Blackwell.

Hopkins, D. and Harris, A. (1997) Improving the quality of education for all, *Support for Learning*, 12 (4): 147–52.

Hopkins, D., Ainscow, M. and West, M. (1994) *School Improvement in an Era of Change*. London, New York: Cassell.

Hopkins, D., Ainscow, M. and West, M. (1996) Unravelling the complexities of school improvement: a case study of the 'Improving the Quality of Education for All' (IQEA) project. Open University Course E838 reader, *Organisational Effectiveness and Improvement in Education*. Buckingham: Open University Press.

Hopkins, D., Harris, A. and Jackson, D. (1997a) Understanding the school's capacity for development: growth states and strategies, *School Leadership and Management*, 17 (3): 401–11.

Hopkins, D., West, M., Ainscow, M., Harris, A. and Beresford, J. (1997b) *Creating the Classroom Conditions for School Improvement*. London: David Fulton.

Hopkins, D., West, M. and Beresford, J. (1998) Creating the conditions for classroom and teacher development, *Teachers and Teaching: Theory and Practice*, 4 (1): 115–41.

Hoyle, E. (1986) *The Politics of School Management*. London: Hodder and Stoughton.

Huselid, M.A. (1995) The impact of human resource management: an agenda for the 1990s, *International Journal of Human Resource Management*, 1 (1): 17–43.

Hycner, R.H. (1985) Some guidelines for the phenomenological analysis of interview data, *Human Studies*, 8: 279–303.

Jackson, D., Raymond, L., Weatherill, L. and Fielding, M. (1998) Students as researchers. Paper presented at the International Congress on School Effectiveness and School Improvement, Manchester, January.

Jackson, P.W., Boostrom, R.E. and Hansen, D.T. (1993) *The Moral Life of Schools*. San Francisco, CA: Jossey-Bass.

James, M. (1998) Listening to children, *Economic and Social Research Council Newsletter*, April.

Kotter, J.P. (1990) What leaders really do, *Harvard Business Review*, 90 (3): 24–32.

Krueger, R.A. (1994) *Focus Groups*. London: Sage.

Labour Party (1997) *New Labour. Because Britain Deserves Better*. London: Labour Party.

Lamb, C. (1990) Why headteachers are now facing a learning curve, *Financial Times*, 4 June.

Lazarsfeld, P.F. (1972) *Qualitative Analysis*. Boston: Allyn and Bacon.

Leithwood, K. (1992) The move towards transformational leadership, *Educational Leadership*, 45 (5): 8–12.

Leithwood, K. (1994) Leadership for school restructuring, *Educational Administration Quarterly*, 30 (4): 498–518.

Leithwood, K., Begley, P. and Cousins, B. (1992) *Developing Expert Leadership for Future Schools*. London: Falmer.

Leithwood, K. and Jantzi, D. (1990) Transformational leadership: how principals can help reform cultures, *School Effectiveness and School Improvement*, 1 (4): 249–80.

Leithwood, K., Jantzi, D. and Steinbach, R. (1999) *Changing Leadership for Changing Times*. Buckingham: Open University Press.

Levin, B. (1994) Improving educational productivity through a focus on learners, *Studies in Educational Administration*, 60: 15–21.

Lincoln, Y. and Guba, E. (1985) *Naturalistic Enquiry*. Beverly Hills, CA: Sage.

Lofland, J. (1971) *Analyzing Social Settings*. Belmont, CA: Wadsworth Publishing Company.

Louis, K.S., Marks, H.M. and Kruse, S. (1994) Teachers' professional community in restructuring schools. Paper prepared at the Centre on Organisation and Restructuring of Schools, University of Wisconsin-Madison.

MacBeath, J. (ed.) (1998) *Effective School Leadership: Responding to Change*. London: Paul Chapman.

MacDuffie, J.P. (1995) Human resource bundles and manufacturing performance: flexible production systems in the world auto industry, *Industrial Relations and Labor Review*, 48: 197–221.

MacGilchrist, B., Mortimore, P., Savage, J. and Beresford, C. (1995) *Planning Matters. The Impact of Development Planning in Primary Schools*. London: Paul Chapman.

McLaughlin, M.W. (1993) What matters most in teachers' workplace context?, in J.W. Little and M.W. McLaughlin (eds) *Teachers' Work: Individuals, Colleagues and Contexts*. New York: Teachers College Press.

McNally, P. and Patching, B. (1994) Principal as facilitator of effective learning and teaching: towards a school-based action plan. Mimeo, James Cook University of North Queensland.

Maden, M. and Rudduck, J. (1997) Listen to the learners, *Times Educational Supplement*, 4 July.

Mahony, P. and Hextall, I. (1997) Problems of accountability in reinvented government: a case study of the Teacher Training Agency, *Journal of Educational Policy*, 12 (4): 267–78.

Mapstone, R. (1990) Staff management and the school principal, in E. Cave and C. Wilkinson (eds) *Local Management of Schools. Some Practical Issues*. London: Routledge.

Marzano, R.J., Arredondo, D.E., Brandt, R.S., Pickering, D.J., Blackburn, G.J. and Moffett, C.A. (1992) *Dimensions of Learning*. Teacher's Manual. Aurora, CO: Association for Supervision and Curriculum Development/Mid-continent Regional Educational Laboratory Institute.

Maykut, P. and Morehouse, R. (1994) *Beginning Qualitative Research: A Philosophic and Practical Guide*. London: Falmer.

Meece, J.L. and Miller, S.D. (1996) Developmental changes in children's self-reports of achievement goals, competence, and strategy use during the late elementary years. Paper presented at AERA Annual Conference, New York, April.

Miles, M.B. and Huberman, A.M. (1984) *Qualitative Data Analysis: A Sourcebook of New Methods*. Beverly Hills, CA: Sage.

Miles, M.B. and Huberman, A.M. (1994) *Qualitative Data Analysis: An Expanded Sourcebook*. Thousand Oaks, CA: Sage.

Mintzberg, H. (1994) *The Rise and Fall of Strategic Planning*. New York: Free Press.

Moisan, C. (1990) Local management of schools: implications for teachers, in C. Gilbert (ed.) *Local Management of Schools. A Guide for Governors and Teachers*. London: Kogan Page.

Morgan, C. and Morris, G. (1999) *Good Teaching and Learning: Pupils and Teachers Speak*. Buckingham: Open University Press.

Morgan, D.L. (1988) *Focus Groups as Qualitative Research*. London: Sage.

Morgan, G. (1993) *Images of Organization*. London: Sage.

Mortimore, P. and Mortimore, J. (eds) (1991) *The Primary Head. Roles, Responsibilities and Reflections*. London: Paul Chapman.

Mortimore, P., Sammons, P., Stoll, L., Lewis, D. and Ecob, R. (1988) *School Matters*. Wells: Open Books.

Mortimore, P., Sammons, P., Stoll, L., Lewis, D. and Ecob, R. (1994) Key factors for effective junior schooling, in A. Pollard and J. Bourne (eds) *Teaching and Learning in the Primary School*. London: Routledge.

Newman, E. (1997) Children's views of school – a vehicle for developing teaching practice. Paper presented at BERA Annual Conference, York, September.

Nias, J., Southworth, G. and Yeomans, R. (1989) *Staff Relationships in the Primary School: A Study of School Culture*. London: Cassell.

Nightingale, D. (1988) LFM profits. Letter in *Times Educational Supplement*, 10 June.

Noddings, N. (1992) *The Challenge to Care in Schools*. New York: Teachers College Press.

Norwich, B. (1998) Developing an inventory of children's class learning approaches, *Educational Psychology in Practice*, 14 (3): 147–55.

OECD (1994) *Quality in Education*. Paris: Organization for Economic Co-operation and Development.

Ofsted (Office for Standards in Education) (1995) *The Annual Report of Her Majesty's Chief Inspector of Schools: Standards and Quality in Education*. London: HMSO.

Ofsted (Office for Standards in Education)/UBI (Understanding British Industry)/Unilever/DfE (Department for Education) (1995) *Developing Senior Managers. Summary Report*. London: Ofsted.

Osborn, M. (1997) Learning, working and climbing the ladder: pupil perspectives on primary schooling in England and France. Paper presented at the European Conference on Educational Research, Frankfurt, September.

Patterson, M.G., West, M.A., Lawthom, R. and Nickell, S. (1997) *Impact of People Management Practices on Business Performance*. London: Institute of Personnel and Development.

Patton, M.Q. (1980) *Qualitative Evaluation Methods*. Beverly Hills, CA: Sage.

Patton, M.Q. (1990) *Qualitative Evaluation and Research Methods*, 2nd ed. Beverly Hills, CA: Sage.

Peters, R.S. (ed.) (1976) *The Role of the Head*. London: Routledge and Kegan Paul.

Pipes, M. (1988) Digesting delegation, *Education*, 19 August.

Pollard, A., Broadfoot, P., Croll, P., Osborn, M. and Abbot, D. (1994) *Changing English Primary Schools? The Impact of the Educational Reform Act at Key Stage One*. London: Cassell.

Pollard, H.R. (1978) *Further Developments in Management Thought*. London: William Heinemann.

Reeves, J., Mahoney, P. and Moos, L. (1997) Headship: issues of career, *Teacher Development*, 1 (1): 43–56.

Restructuring Collaborative (1997) *Look Who's Talking Now. Student Views of Learning in Restructuring Schools*. Portland, OR: Regional Educational Laboratory Network.

Reynolds, D. (1991) Changing ineffective schools, in M. Ainscow (ed.) *Effective Schools For All*. London: David Fulton.

Ribbins, P. (1993) Conversations with a condottiere of administrative value, *Journal of Educational Administration and Foundations*, 8 (1): 24–32.

Ribbins, P. (1996) Heads and headship today: waving or drowning?, *Forum*, 38 (1): 24–5.

Ribbins, P. and Sherratt, B. (1992) Managing the secondary school in the 1990s: a new view of headship, *Educational Management and Administration*, 20 (3): 151–60.

Riley, K. and Mahoney, P. (1995) Heads you win, heads you lose, *Times Educational Supplement*, 6 October.

Riseborough, G. (1993) Primary headship, state policy and the challenge of the 1990s: an exceptional story that disproves total hegemonic rule, *Journal of Education Policy*, 8 (2): 155–73.

Rosener, J.B. (1990) Ways women lead, *Harvard Business Review*, November/December.

Rosenholtz, S. (1989) *Teachers' Workplace: The Social Organisation of Schools*. New York: Longman.

Rudduck, J. (1991) *Innovation and Change: Developing Involvement and Understanding*. Buckingham: Open University Press.

Rudduck, J., Chaplain, R. and Wallace, G. (eds) (1996a) *School Improvement: What Can Pupils Tell Us?* London: David Fulton.

Rudduck, J., Chaplain, R. and Wallace, G. (1996b) Pupils' voices and school improvement, in J. Rudduck, R. Chaplain and G. Wallace (eds) *School Improvement: What Can Pupils Tell Us?* London: David Fulton.

Rutter, M., Maughan, B., Mortimore, P. and Ouston, J. (1979) *Fifteen Thousand Hours: Secondary Schools and their Effects on Children.* London: Open Books.

Sammons, P., Hillman, J. and Mortimore, P. (1995) *Key Characteristics of Effective Schools: A Review of School Effectiveness Research.* London: Office for Standards in Education and Institute of Education, University of London.

Sammons, P., Thomas, S. and Mortimore, P. (1996) Promoting school and departmental effectiveness, *Management in Education,* 10: 22–4.

Sammons, P., Thomas, S. and Mortimore, P. (1997) *Forging Links: Effective Schools and Effective Departments.* London: Paul Chapman.

Saunders, T. (1987) Adding up the problems, *Junior Education,* July: 12–13.

Schatzman, L. and Strauss, A.L. (1973) *Field Research: Strategies for a Natural Sociology.* Englewood Cliffs, NJ: Prentice Hall.

Scheerens, J. (1992) *School Effectiveness.* London: Cassell.

Scottish Consultative Council on the Curriculum (1996) *Teaching for Effective Learning.* Dundee: Scottish CCC.

Senge, P. (1990) *The Fifth Discipline.* New York: Doubleday.

Sergiovanni, T.J. (1992) *Moral Leadership: Getting to the Heart of School Improvement.* San Francisco, CA: Jossey-Bass.

Sergiovanni, T.J. (1995) *The Principalship: A Reflective Practice Perspective.* Boston, MA: Allyn and Bacon.

Sergiovanni, T.J. (1998) Leadership as pedagogy, capital development and school effectiveness, *International Journal of Leadership in Education,* 1 (1): 37–47.

Shakeshaft, C. (1989) *Women in Educational Administration.* California: Corwin Press Inc.

Shimahara, N. (1990) Anthroethnography: a methodological consideration, in R.R. Sherman and R.B. Webb (eds) *Qualitative Research in Education: Focus and Methods.* London: Falmer.

Siegel, P. and Byrne, S. (1994) *Using Quality to Redesign School Systems: The Cutting Edge of Common Sense.* San Francisco, CA: Jossey-Bass.

Sizer, J. (1989) *An Insight into Management Accounting.* London: Penguin.

Slee, R., Weiner, G. and Tomlinson, S. (1998) *School Effectiveness for Whom?* London: Falmer.

Smees, R. and Thomas, S. (1998) Valuing pupils' views about school, *British Journal of Curriculum and Assessment,* 8 (3): 7–9.

Smith, M.S., Scoll, B.W. and Link, J. (1996) Research-based school reform: the Clinton administration's agenda, in E.A. Hanushek and D.W. Jorgenson (eds) *Improving America's Schools: The Role of Incentives.* Washington, DC: National Academy Press.

Sockett, H. (1993) *The Moral Base for Teacher Professionalism*. New York: Teachers College Press.

SooHoo, S. (1993) Students as partners in research and restructuring schools, *The Educational Forum*, 57: 386–92.

Southworth, G. (1990) Leadership, headship and effective primary schools, *School Organisation*, 10 (1): 3–16.

Southworth, G. (1993) School leadership and school development: reflections from research, *School Organisation*, 13 (1): 73–87.

Southworth, G. (1995) *Talking Heads: Voices of Experience*. Cambridge: University of Cambridge Institute of Education.

Southworth, G. (1996) Improving primary schools: shifting the emphasis and clarifying the focus, *School Organisation*, 16 (3): 263–80.

Southworth, G., Pocklington, K. and Weindling, D. (1998) *A Qualitative Study of Headship in Primary, Secondary and Special Schools*. Haywards Heath: National Association of Headteachers.

Staessens, K. and Vandenburghe, R. (1994) Vision as a core component in school culture, *Journal of Curriculum Studies*, 26 (2): 187–200.

Stoll, L. and Fink, D. (1996) *Changing our Schools*. London: Open University Press.

Strain, M. (1990) Resource management in schools: some conceptual and practical considerations, in E. Cave and C. Wilkinson (eds) *Local Management of Schools. Some Practical Issues*. London: Routledge.

Summers, A.A. and Johnson, A.W. (1996) The effects of school-based management plans, in E.A. Hanushek and D.W. Jorgenson (eds) *Improving America's Schools: The Role of Incentives*. Washington, DC: New Academy Press.

Tagg, H. (1986) Control of the purse strings, *Times Educational Supplement*, 14 November.

Talbert, J.E. and McLaughlin, M. (1994) Teacher professionalism in local school contexts, *American Journal of Education*, 102: 123–53.

Tampoe, M. (1998) *Liberating Leadership*. London: The Industrial Society.

Taylor, F.W. (1911) *The Principles of Scientific Management*. New York: Harper.

Taylor, W. (1976) The head as manager: some criticisms, in R.S. Peters (ed.) *The Role of the Head*. London: Routledge and Kegan Paul.

Teacher Training Agency (1996) *Consultation Paper on Training for Serving Headteachers*. London: Teacher Training Agency.

Teacher Training Agency (1997) *National Standards for Headteachers*. London: Teacher Training Agency.

Teacher Training Agency (1998) *Leadership Programme for Serving Headteachers*. London: Teacher Training Agency.

Teacher Training Agency (1999) *National Professional Qualification for Headteachers*. London: Teacher Training Agency.

Telford, H. (1996) *Transforming Schools through Collaborative Leadership*. London: Falmer.

Tesch, R. (1990) *Qualitative Research: Analysis Types and Software Tools.* Basingstoke: Falmer.

Thomas, H. (1987) Efficiency and opportunity in school finance autonomy, in H. Thomas and T. Simkins *Economics and the Management of Education: Emerging Themes.* London: Falmer.

Tom, A. (1984) *Teaching as a Moral Craft.* New York: Longman.

Troman, G. (1996) Headteachers, collaborative school cultures and school improvement: a changing relationship?, *Educational Action Research*, 4 (1): 119–44.

Turner, B.A. (1981) Some practical aspects of qualitative data analysis: one way of organising the cognitive process associated with the generation of grounded theory, *Quality and Quantity*, 15: 225–47.

van Manen, M. (1977) Linking ways of knowing to ways of being practical, *Curriculum Inquiry*, 6 (3): 205–28.

van Velzen, W., Miles, M., Ekholm, M., Haymeyer, U. and Robin, D. (1985) *Making School Improvement Work.* Leuven, Belgium: ACCO.

Vroom, V.H. and Deci, E.L. (eds) (1989) *Management and Motivation. Selected Readings.* London: Penguin.

Walker, R. (ed.) (1989) *Applied Qualitative Research.* Aldershot: Gower.

Wallace, G. (1996) Relating to teachers, in J. Rudduck, R. Chaplain and G. Wallace (eds) *School Improvement: What Can Students Tell Us?* London: David Fulton.

Wallace, J. and Wildy, H. (1996) Old questions for new schools: what are the students doing? Paper presented at the AERA (American Research Association) Annual Conference, New York.

Wallace, M. (1991) Coping with multiple innovations: an exploratory study, *School Organisation*, 11 (2): 187–209.

Wallace, M. and Hall, V. (1994) *Inside the SMT: Teamwork in Secondary School Management.* London: Paul Chapman.

West-Burnham, J. (1997) *Managing Quality in Schools.* London: Pitman.

Wilkinson, C. (1990) The management of time, in E. Cave and C. Wilkinson (eds) *Local Management of Schools. Some Practical Issues.* London: Routledge.

Woods, P. (1993) *Critical Events in Teaching and Learning.* London: Falmer.

Yin, R. (1989) *Case Study Research: Design and Methods,* London: Sage.

INDEX